The Best of You
vs
The Rest of You

A Path to
WHOYOUBEING?

MELVIN D. FOREMAN

Thank
Ms. Vickie,
for your unsolicited
warmth, kindness and
top notch assistance. I don't
know where I would be without folk
like you helping to pull me along.
may the Best of your life be the rest of your life.

Sincerely!

Melvin D. Foreman

ISBN: 1542815533
ISBN-13: 978-1542815536

Library of Congress Control Number: 2017910168
CreateSpace Independent Publishing Platform, North Charleston, SC

DEDICATION

This book is dedicated to my mother and father, Frances Martha James Foreman, and William Miles Foreman who loved each other dearly and shared that love with us. To my sister Mary, and my identical twin brother Marvin, who have challenged me to be my *Best* growing up and continue to do so today. To my wife LaMonica, who has been my constant support regardless of what path, idea, or project I've pursued. To Douglas Collins; my cousin and a great man who lost his life to a senseless act of domestic violence. To the countless other friends and associates; who left us too soon, at the hands of violence, abuse or dysfunction. To my current and former students who have allowed me to coach, teach, and share my living philosophy with them on and off the tennis court. I am committed to sharing my living philosophy with some of the insight contained in this book, *The Best of You vs The Rest of You*. Our Best is yet to come.

TABLE OF CONTENTS

FOREWORD

It's been said that life is a question and how we live our lives is the answer. Melvin "Coach" Foreman, author and dynamic speaker, has written a powerful life transforming book entitled *The Best of You vs The Rest of You, a Path to WhoyouBeing?* This thought provoking, mind expanding concept, challenges all of us to live our lives from the inside out to create the greatest version of ourselves mentally, emotionally and in every dimension of our lives. Melvin has spent the majority of his life inspiring our youth and now he's created a new chapter in his life, inspired by slogans he observed on the t-shirts of young people in his native city of Detroit. One day in the moment of spiritual insight, the thought of the profound title of this life changing masterpiece that goes beyond positive thinking and motivation, dropped into his spirit. Melvin in each chapter touches and impacts the core of our very being. This book encourages us to face the man in the mirror to answer the question *"WhoyouBeing?* how are you showing up in life?" This book as you will find will transform your life as it has mine. I encourage you to read it from cover to cover. Melvin, you've done good, you are a positive example for all of us. You have greatness within you and each chapter is a manifestation of that greatness.

—Les Brown, author of *Live Your Dreams,*
It's Not Over Until You Win

ACKNOWLEDGMENTS

I would like to express my love and gratitude to the following people: Lisa Thomas for the numerous times we met and went over ideas and concepts ultimately used in writing the book.

Linda McIntosh, my neighbor, along with Vickie Baker and Stacy Brooks, the librarians who assisted me with editing the book.

D' Andre Herron, who unselfishly provided his computer and creative tech savvy to design, and redesign the book cover and content numerous times until we settled on the one used.

La Monica, my wife, for putting up with me and my way of being throughout this process.

Bettie Barton, my spiritual mentor, who I may not see for long periods of time but her influence, is forever with me.

To Carol Brown who consistently allowed me to bounce book related ideas off of her; along with everyone else not singled out but who did provide some type of assistance with the development, writing and completion of the book.

To the countless number of folk who continuously asked about the book, and when it would be completed.

Last but not least, all the people I was able to learn from over the years that stood and still stand for the existence of a wonderful, loving, and purposeful world. I love and appreciate you all.

INTRODUCTION

The Only True Challenges We Have in Life Are The Ones That Take Place within Us. Over the past couple of years as I traveled to different venues in Detroit, I began to notice a new phenomenon – a written attitude among Detroiters. "Us versus Everybody," or "Detroit vs Everybody," expressed on t-shirts being worn around the city. I began seeing similar t-shirts with particular high schools vs everybody on them. I thought to myself, "what are they feeling or trying to convey?" My mind wondered into a deep trance and emerged with a new twist. What a wonderful way to introduce everybody to a way of thinking that could transform our lives and way of being. By changing the context of the message we could alter our thoughts and impact our living experience.

I thought about how the original intent of the sayings may have been to create some kind of team unity or sense of pride within the city or particular high school. However, if we changed the wording to *"The Best of You vs The Rest of You"* we could signify that our greatest challenge and need for unity abides within us. We could actively challenge ourselves to live from our inner, highest level of *Self,* and model that level for one another. This could change the way we see each other, the way we live, witness and experience life. *The Best of Us* emanates from within us, and does not reflect less than loving activities outside of us.

This "Detroit vs Everybody" caught my attention because I knew that our biggest and primary challenge in life is not versus other people, places or things but strictly with a less than our *Best* side within us. If we would allow *the Best of Us* to prevail internally, we could change the face of ourselves, and society externally. Initially, I thought I would create t-shirts which read *"The Best of You vs The Rest of You"*; then the idea morphed from a phrase on a t-shirt to a living philosophy I would share and the title of this book.

This book is an introduction to me, my experience, education and journey; a transformed life that saved and set me free. It speaks to my story, who I am, where I'm from and who I've become; living, loving and sharing my life. I have lived both a wonderful and not so wonderful life of love.

It's about my pursuit of a recipe for happiness beginning at age ten or eleven; things I found, learned, and applied along the way. It encompasses the principles, practices and the people I met; thoughts, ideas and things I regret. It contains the challenging days and winning ways I've experienced and have come to know.

I will highlight where I transitioned between being lost and seeking, found awareness, accepted a new view, actively changed to a new way of being and winning.

This book is written to bring attention to the energy and power of *Self*, where it comes from, and what we can do with it to change the course of our lives. Your success from reading this book will be determined by the choices you make, habits you develop and your commitment to choosing *the Best of You over the Rest of You*.

For clarification purposes, the term *the Best of You* refers to you living the God in you, *the Christ* in you and your highest expression of *Self*.

It's:

- You living the highest qualities and *Love* in you.
- You living from the foundation of *Creation* and *Source of Supply*.
- You embracing *He* who created *the Heavens and the Earth*, and has the last say in how your life will unfold.

The term *the Rest of You* refers to you living less than *the Best of You*, attached to a way of thinking which keeps you high and dry (in the worst way).

It's:

- Your life being driven by negative thoughts, feelings or emotions.
- You being led by symptoms of fear such as hate, anger, and envy.
- You living focused on past pain, problems, and personalities.
- You putting what you have, what you do, and how you sometimes feel before, who you are, or your being.
- A combination of your *Average* and *Worst Self*.

This book is an inspirational memoir about my life's journey from violence and abuse to living my truth at the level of a transformed life. A wonderful life through mental toughness, mindfulness, and the daily practice of *Best*.

Where are you, and where do you want to be? We all possess *the Best and the Rest* of qualities. The success of living *the Best of You* is achieved through awareness, acceptance, active engagement and change when needed at any moment in your life. The distinction between *the Best and the Rest of you* will be further conveyed throughout the book.

Expressed is my strongest desire to share and support love, personal power, and what we so often forget; our *Purpose* in life.

It is our living *Purpose* to remember who we really are, why we are here, what we love and have come here to do. When we do this, we can live, enjoy and share a life of love, individually and collectively.

I grew up with a burning desire to understand human beings. I wanted to find out what I could do to help turn around our unpredictable, unkind, unloving world. I made it a personal challenge to help eliminate the violence, abuse and dysfunction in my community and communities around the world. I have found that in order to do so I must eradicate the less than loving characteristics within myself. Unless we go within and heal, we will never heal what's outside of us. The *Self* within provides us with our greatest challenges and rewards. We must begin within to forge a life of love, and live it more abundantly.

As a young black male, I grew up as a redheaded twin, Melvin D. Foreman, with my identical brother, Marvin, my sister named Mary and our mother Frances Martha James Foreman.

My father, William Miles Foreman, passed away when I was 4. A few years after his death, our family of four moved to the Sojourner Truth Projects, a low-income housing complex on the eastside of Detroit, where I spent the rest of my childhood. Growing up black, fatherless and living in low income housing made it easy to define myself as less than. The purposeful, powerful person that I accepted for myself came later. I am now and have always been a child of God, a *Kingdom kid*, an individualized expression of *Love and greatness*, here on the planet with a powerful purpose to be; something I didn't understand or claim as a child.

We are bigger, better, and greater than any role, position, label or social status we can have, give or obtain. I've come to accept that if I can live *the Best of Me* in spite of my life and *the Rest of Me*, so can you. I submit to you that there is a direct correlation between the *Level of Self* you live from, and the experience of life you have. If you want to experience *the Best of Life*, live *the Best of You. The Best of You* is best; *the Rest* is just your test.

I will share some stories of struggle living stuck in a cultural mentality of past pain, problems, pitfalls, frustration, and uncertainty. I will share situations and problems viewed and dealt with initially from the space of *the Rest of Me*; and then eventual victories after shifting and living from the perspective and space of *the Best of Me*.

Definiteness of purpose, effort and commitment are instrumental on our journey moving forward. Many of us say we want wonderful change in our lives but are not willing to do the necessary work to have that change take place. I'm encouraging you to take a good look at where you are and where you want to be. The "same old same old" *Rest of You* still wants you and wants to control you; while "the life you love" *Best of You* awaits you. At any given moment of your life you can choose to be and live from the *Best of You*.

This book will help you recognize when you are practicing *the Best of You* and when you are not. Take it upon yourself to read, listen, learn, and apply the principles, methods, and ways representing *the Best of You* shown throughout the book. Commit yourself to an ongoing practice, then "lovingly live a life you love" can be your own reality.

The first six chapters in the book are a chronological account of the journey I took to learn, accept, and experience principles and a living philosophy that worked and led me to the space of *Best*. The last three chapters are used to explain my recipe for happiness, *"WhoyouBeing?"* and *Best Self Living*.

This book concludes with a recap of my journey, systems and methods I used, and ways you can do so as well.

I trust this book will help you express *the Best of You*, and to lovingly live a life you love in spite of *the Rest of You*. It's your choice, your voice, and you get to choose.

Let's begin; *Best Self Living* starts now. *#WhoyouBeing?*

CHAPTER 1

IS THIS THE WAY IT IS?

"No way, I don't believe it, you've got to be kidding," were my words that hot summer evening, when I first heard that the beautiful twenty something year old lady who lived a few doors down from us had been shot to death by her husband.

I must have been about ten years old when it happened. I was in disbelief; how could her husband and father of their three young children do such a thing to someone he was supposed to love. When I thought about it, she had been in that abusive relationship with him for at least a few years; the amount of time they had lived down the street. So often she was seen in their front yard or on the front porch with visible signs of physical abuse. Their relationship was definitely a volatile one.

I remember the stories about how her husband had pushed her down the flight of stairs that separated the first and second floors where they lived. She was such an attractive woman. I just wanted to rescue her from the violent outbreaks that seemed to occur so often. I didn't know how; I was just a kid. I simply observed with sadness, shock and disbelief, and now she was gone. *(Lost and seeking)*

Given the neighborhood we grew up in and the mentality of the people there, it seemed hard, if not impossible, to live a life of love. Based on what most of us saw each day; we did not have many uplifting role models, examples or clues on how to live better than we did. Many of us had lost hope and faith in anything other than how it was or had been.

We grew up in a culture that focused so much on the mighty dollar, the pursuit of financial wealth and riches, that we as a people were losing ourselves, family, friends, and loved ones. Violence, abuse and dysfunction ran rampant not only in our society, cities, communities and families; but basically in all of our relationships to one degree or another. We as a culture had seemingly lost our way and if we didn't make a shift to turn things around, there would be nothing left worth spending our money on regardless of the amount we accumulated.

Forty plus years later we share a very similar story. The problems, concerns and issues that were taking place then are still happening today only at a higher rate; be it in our homes, workplaces, schools, and communities or the widening gap between the rich and the poor.

We can talk about:
a) the violence in our streets and how our justice system does not appear to be working for us
b) our institutions and the corruption that has taken place in recent years
c) the crash on Wall Street in 2008, and the horrible impact it had on our economy and so many people
d) the lack of police officers, firefighters, EMS workers, and the conditions in which they work

e) the increasing duties and responsibilities of workers in the workplace and the shrinking of wages and benefits at the same time

f) the healthcare system, costs, and unhealthy conditions of so many people which puts a strain on them and our economy

g) the ongoing wars we fight both here in the United States and abroad; and the list goes on

At this point in time on the planet, it seems as if a majority of us have forgotten who we really are, why we are here, and what we were created to do. So many people are stuck in a cloud, walking around lost, feeling hopeless, helpless about their lives and life in general.

Human beings build, make, and create things every day. We see a need and we fill it. We have spent such a large part of our lives working to acquire and accumulate material things, while lacking

time, energy and effort spent on developing and progressing the most important resource that we have which is *Self*, the essence of who we really are. *Self* at the forefront of our cultural mind would provide us with both meaningful products and create wonderful, kind, caring people able to procreate, and raise children who become more loving, beautiful, purposeful people. We would not put things before people or fear before love.

The amount of time spent on understanding and living our *Higher Self* has been deficient, and because of this, our lives individually and collectively have suffered. The ill wills of our society stem from this lack of knowing and living as our true selves.

When you don't know how to lovingly live a life you love, you miss out on living your truest hopes, dreams, and purpose. You deny yourself living, lasting, loving relationships. You rob your friends, family, and loved ones of wonderful sustaining years of happiness. When you don't know how to live this way, you die without experiencing what was rightfully yours to have. You don't get to live, love, learn and leave a legacy of joy and happiness to those you care for so deeply. You never get to experience life at the level you were meant to. *(Awareness)*

My personal journey included people who were showing me how awful life can be, and others how beautiful living life is. I was committed to going out and finding a recipe for happiness; I did, and I am eager to share it with you. There were a few living philosophies I picked up and accepted for myself which came from my wonderful mother Frances Martha James Foreman. Expressions and insight such as:

- Do your best at whatever you do, regardless of the type of work.
- Don't hate anyone.
- We're the richest poor folk in the world.
- Your father was a small piece of leather, but well put together; the apple of my eye and I loved him dearly. *(Acceptance)*

Mother kept us busy. She had us involved in all types of recreation, athletic and extracurricular activities. From swimming to softball, baseball, roller skating, archery, bowling, tennis, summer camp, we were there. We were the richest poor folk in the world. We didn't have a lot of money, fancy clothes or cars, but we had a lot of love and exposure to a variety of activities.

My father passed when I was 4, yet he was a role model for me. Growing up I didn't remember a lot about him; however, because of the information my mother shared with me about him, I wanted to be like my father when I grew up. So often she would speak about how good of a man he was. Sober or intoxicated she would express her love for my father. My mother did one heck of a job raising my older sister, myself and my twin brother as a single mother.

One summer afternoon a few months before my 11th birthday, a good friend of my mother and our family, told me, "You need to be the man of the house and take care of your mother, sister and brother." Over the years he had made it a point to help my mother with presents on our birthdays and holidays. However, he was letting me know things were going to be different and I needed to step up.

I accepted the responsibility; but felt I had no choice. I was born twenty minutes before my twin brother Marvin, which made me the oldest male and technically the man of the house. I said yes to the necessary mental shift in my thinking, but at the same time had no idea how to fulfill my new inherited responsibility. Ours was just another fatherless home where a young male had been told to be the man and take care of the family when he's just a kid and barely knows how to take care of himself. It's just the way it is, I thought.

I was already the type of kid who would think things through; and had already shouldered some responsibilities; this basically took my thinking and concern to another level. *(Acceptance)*

While this was going on in my house, the attitude and community mindset was pretty much the same, stuck in a painful past of negative attitudes and hostile ways. Fun times did take place; they just seemed to be overshadowed by the unpleasant things associated with them. Living for the weekend was definitely a norm in the community. Many, if not most people, were working on jobs they didn't necessarily care for but did anyway because the job provided income and money to pay bills and whatever else was needed to get by.

The lack of true love for their work helped fuel the living for the weekend mentality. It was our way of life to spend Friday and Saturday nights listening to music, dancing, drinking and playing cards at a social gathering in the neighborhood. It made sense that people would look forward to the weekend gatherings but what didn't make sense to me was how problems and violence seemed to stem from them.

"Mr. Grant is going to get his gun, get away from the windows" my mother said, as she came in the front door returning from one of the parties down the street on this particular Friday night. "Again?" one of my siblings or I expressed. "Every time you look around mom he's going to get his gun." "Who is it this time, Rodney again?" "Yes it is," she said, "You know Mr. Grant doesn't like anyone mistreating women, and definitely not in front of him, drunk or sober." A few minutes later a shot or two rang out and the party was over. Everyone who hadn't left already was leaving. It was almost an every other weekend party ritual. I didn't like it.

Violence, abuse and dysfunction lived in the Sojourner Truth Housing Projects; it was common practice in the neighborhood. It represented a state of mind many people in the community grew up with. I did not think true happiness would be an experience of ours at the rate we were going. Too many people were living stuck in a painful past; a self-defeating place where negative attitudes and hostile ways grew daily. There had to be another way. This led me to seek answers. Many folks wanted a different experience but they didn't know what to do or how to go about it. This book will share some answers. *(Living Lost)*

I was eleven years old, still being a kid but conscientious and concerned about being a good man of the house. I wanted to live in a more enjoyable, refreshing, safe and stable kind of neighborhood.

I don't know what it was about this particular day but I took it upon myself to ask some kids and adults, "What would it take for you to be happy in life?" The resounding answer I got back was "If I had a million dollars I'd be happy." I felt I would be happy too if we had a million dollars. However, what I really wanted to know was a way to be happy without it; just in case we never got it. There had to be a way to be happy, without a million dollars being a prerequisite. I made it my mission to find the answer. *(Lost and seeking)*

I developed a shy sort of personality after I met my so called first love at the age of 13 in middle school. It was the kind of love at first sight you hear about in Fairy tales and old romantic movies. She simply looked like the woman of my dreams, and all I wanted was for her to feel the same about me. It appeared that she did for a while at least, or so I thought. Then, out of the blue she dumped me. The night of our high school Homecoming dance she called it quits. No reason or explanation was given then or later. All I wanted to know at that point was why, why, why?

After a few weeks, I accepted that I was not going to get a reason or answer from her, and it simply left me dumbfounded. What could have happened, what could I have done to make her start and then stop loving or wanting me? I was devastated, continuously asking myself, why, why, why, why me? I fell into a silent funk; but didn't share my blues with anyone. Day in and day out, as I carried on among friends and family as normal as can be, on the inside I was torn apart.

I found myself enrolled in school that summer. I had received a "D" in two classes that school year and that was unacceptable. Instead of doing classwork I had spent a lot of time thinking and wondering why she left me and what if. The time not paying attention in class did not serve me well, so I spent the hot summer mornings in school rather than home outside playing with my twin brother and friends. It was not an enjoyable eight weeks of summer school at all.

Although my answer to the ongoing question of why she left never got answered, I did make a vow to never fall for a girl so hard ever again. Never to the point where I could not function at a sensible level and continue to take care of my responsibilities if something were to cause us to break up.

I moved on from that lost relationship but was more guarded with my feelings and thinking. Her rejection was something I may have managed, but it was not something I wanted to go through again. My trust and confidence with girls began to decrease so much that even though I was talkative around friends and family, I became quite the quiet type when it came to girls, especially those I did not know very well. I imagine I became this guy as a way of avoiding the feeling of rejection I had come to know.

Over a period of time my behavior fit the description of what shy was, so I unknowingly accepted that definition as truth for myself and simply learned to live with it.

As I grew older in my teenage years, I continued to focus on life as a whole. I believed there had to be a better way; and I wanted to find it. I didn't want to get caught up in what I had been seeing around me day in and day out. I had a dream that was bigger than what I was seeing. My dream was something that would redefine me, my family and community. Becoming a professional quarterback in the National Football League (NFL) would fit the bill. *(Lost and seeking)*

Early on I wanted to be accepted among my peers, but realized my goal to live a successful and happy life as a professional football player would require me to be smoke, alcohol and drug free.

My close friends however were beginning to dabble in those things and being around them I was expected to do so as well. Right from the start there was peer pressure from my friends. I chose to stand up to the pressure, and said no when they insisted that I join in. The harassment lasted for about two weeks and once it was clear I was sticking to my stance the hassling stopped and turned into acceptance and unexpected support.

The power of choosing to live differently awarded me support in remaining drug, alcohol and smoke free. The road was unfamiliar, but one I was able to conquer due to my strong commitment to that which mattered most; one of the qualities in living *the Best of You*.

Being a professional football player in the NFL would have provided me with millions of dollars. Now mind you, there was no guarantee that I would make it into the NFL. However, the idea or possibility that I could, led me to overcome the peer pressure. I stuck to my dream and sense of *Self*, and the peer pressure around me dissolved. (*Awareness, acceptance, active change, and attainment*)

To me, drugs or alcohol would surely have been the downfall of any attempt to be a successful professional athlete. I believed if I accomplished the dream of playing in the NFL, it would give me and my family the opportunity to leave the projects and the day-to-day challenges we faced there.

The millions of dollars everyone was talking about would bring happiness and it would be a reality for me. That's only, if I actually made it into the NFL.

My twin brother and I were pretty popular in school. He was known as the so called "talker" and "bad twin" while I was described as the "good twin." I believed it was a title I was given as a result of my being shy as a teenager.

I enjoyed being called the good twin, however, being shy I did not like. It was simply how and who I thought I was.

We were heavily involved in school sports; I played quarterback on the football team, he played baseball. We both were on the high school swimming team and members of a popular neighborhood drill team, the Royal Knights. I was successful in the various activities but not with the girls.

I eventually got tired of being shy; and sought a better way. I conquered that challenge, but still had others I needed help with. In the upcoming chapter I will share how I took a "Seek and ye shall find" attitude as I traveled through life to find and apply what had been missing or lost. *(Lost, sought and found)*

CHAPTER 2

SEEK AND YE SHALL FIND

I had grown accustomed to defining myself as shy. I had become familiar with the violence, abuse and dysfunction that went on in our community. Both were issues in my life I was hoping could be different. If I could change from being shy to outgoing; that would be progress personally, and finding a way to change the state of our culture would be my recipe for life.

I attended Olivet College, a small college in Michigan; only a couple of hours away from where I grew up. It took high school graduation, four years in college, and my 21st birthday approaching, before I got my 1st glimpse of another way of being; and an answer to what I was looking for, to grow out of my shyness.

It was my senior year of college when I decided that my shyness was not serving me, and I wanted to be different, even though I didn't know how. I was truly sick and tired of being shy. I wished I or someone else knew what to do.

I had developed a way of being that I no longer liked, yet didn't know how to change. It was just my way of life until I began my search for an answer.

I found my answer in a book titled "Your Erroneous Zones," written by Dr. Wayne Dyer, a prominent psychologist at the time. A particular chapter in the book provided me with insight, awareness and a changed view of myself.

By changing my conversation about myself, my behavior changed and I found freedom and, a new way of being I hadn't known before. The book provided the learning moment, life lesson, and growth in love I needed.

At almost 21, after spending some five or more years living as a shy guy; it took a strong desire, an emphatic decision to change, and searching for another way before my answer was found in a book. I changed, made the shyness a thing of my past, and oh what a relief it was!

This newfound insight did not provide an answer to eliminating the violence, abuse and dysfunction I witnessed growing up, but it sure did help me. It provided a glimpse of hope in overcoming my past. *Your Erroneous Zones* changed my life. If you don't want it, leave it, and speak it in past tense. I was able to change my way of being simply by changing the way I saw and spoke of myself. *(Acceptance, active change, and attainment)*

This triumph over my shyness introduced me to a living principle that I had been unaware of, until I read the book. It was a glimpse into a world I was unfamiliar with but looking forward to learning more about.

After attending Olivet College for two years with me, my twin brother Marvin, who had been my best friend and confidant for the first 20 years of my life, left college, joined the Navy, and moved to San Diego, California where he was stationed. Upon graduating I moved there as well to live with him.

Drill team Melvin and Marvin perform in Olivet's Annual Talent Show.

The two years apart created a wedge between us. So much so that we could not come together in a way to work things out like we had done so well in the formative years of our lives.

He had changed, I had changed, and our perspective on life had grown to be different. With that as the new reality, the time had come after three short months of living together, for me to move out and get my own place. I began a new chapter in my life without the customary brotherly love and support.

As a result of our divide, I blamed him for many of the difficulties I felt, experienced and endured for a long time after. It was the first time in my life that I questioned whether or not I was a whole person or truly half of a whole, with my brother being the other half. I questioned if being an identical twin was actually being a half of a whole since identical twins come from the same egg and not two separate eggs as is the case with fraternal twins. I felt incomplete and my only rationale was; I was half of a whole. We had pretty much been inseparable, up until the time he left college and joined the armed services. However, I did not feel this deep sense of emptiness until after our falling out in Southern California. We had been a winning team, a winning combination. In my mind we could accomplish anything when we put our heads together. This however, was something we could not seem to come together on and it was taking a toll on me. I was so angry at him, I couldn't understand. I didn't know who to talk to; I felt only other sets of identical twins would be able to know what I was going through. I felt lost and alone.

Although I had come to a point in my life where I had gotten a glimpse of a living principle; the power of the word, that exposed me to *the Best of Me*; the majority of my life was still spent living from less than my *Best*, or *the Rest of Me*. This way of being not only affected my relationship with my brother but also affected my personal relationships in general.

I was not only living less than my *Best*; I was living in the realm of "right and wrong". A realm many people in our culture live from. It's a realm where we complain, blame, and shame to justify why we're living less than our *Best* in our lives. We engage in the common attitude of "I'm right and you're wrong"; "you're the reason why things are not working", kind of mentality. It's a common practice where we consciously or subconsciously would rather be right and "win" an argument than accept responsibility for the occurrence. Living from our *Best of Self* we could look for a resolution that is not derived or based on right and wrong, but instead, love and commitment to happy strong relations.

Professionally I was working a job serving the community which corresponded with my strong interest in helping to improve the quality of my community; on the other hand I was not making much money doing so. While I found some reward and refuge in my job, the recipe for happiness still eluded me.

I felt good about graduating from college, which made my mother very proud. She had not received a high school diploma at the time. She had stressed the importance of a college education and succeeding in life to all three of her children. She believed, and led me to believe that I would make lots of money when I got my college education. That was not the case for me. My first job out of college paid me half the amount of money friends who did not attend college was making working in the auto factories back home in Detroit.

I was unhappy with many things:
a) The amount of money I was making
b) The student loans I needed to pay back
c) How friends without degrees were earning more money
d) Personal relationships not working, including the one with my twin brother and former best friend
e) I did not have my recipe for happiness

One particular Saturday afternoon while driving down the highway in San Diego, I was scanning the car radio and stumbled upon a station playing a song titled "Be Grateful," by Lynnette Hawkins of the famous gospel group the Hawkins Family. The lyrics of the song not only caught my attention but ultimately helped shift my view about my life in a big way. Instead of me complaining about the headaches and heartaches I was going through since I had been in San Diego, I realized it was important for me to be grateful. If I wanted to have a wonderful life, I needed to stop complaining about what was missing or what I thought was missing, and be thankful for what I had; and so I did and it helped.

I stopped by a record shop that very day and bought the single. While I was there at the shop I found out she was coming to San Diego in a few weeks for a concert, and yes I bought myself a ticket and went.

I listened to "Be Grateful" on a regular basis. It helped me refocus on finding that recipe for happiness I had set out looking for some ten years prior.

My life experience began to improve again. Regardless of my current situation, I was reminded it could always be worst. This allowed me to see my blessings and put me in a state of mind to look for more blessings rather than focus on what appeared to be missing. A shift in my attitude helped create a shift in my focus and experience. *(Awareness and change)*

I changed some habits and still held on to others. I found out that one of my co-workers was a member of a local gospel group and once she heard of my new found interest, she kept me abreast of when her group was performing, as well as when other gospel acts were coming to San Diego. She also shared numerous gospel albums and tapes for my listening and recording pleasure. I became so engrossed in the music and what it represented that I found myself taking popular secular love songs and changing the lyrics to express love for the Creator and His son, Jesus. I couldn't believe it, but I was giving thanks on a regular basis for the blessings in my life, regardless of what appeared to be missing at the time. As I went clubbing and dancing two or three times a week, I was thanking God and Jesus for my blessings. I was being grateful and living with an attitude of gratitude.

Over the course of the next two years, my life was okay. However, I wasn't living a life I loved, but I was grateful. While the people around me didn't seem to be very positive, I tried to live a happy and fulfilling life. Be that as it may, I still hadn't mended the relationship with my brother.

I continued on my grateful path; and one day in 1982 I met Jean. She seemed like a pleasant person, and she was definitely different than the people I had come to know since moving to San Diego.

I was doing fine on my job, but still wasn't faring well when it came to having a steady girlfriend. I felt having a young lady in my life who was interested in a committed relationship would make a huge difference in my life. Jean was older and of a different persuasion. I liked her and she seemed to like me. We talked and talked, spent time together and I was fascinated with her. She was such a naturally pleasant and joyful person. It was different and unique for me, but I went with it. Her way of being was refreshing and so different at the same time.

I was hesitant about taking it beyond the level of friendship, which it had been for at least six months. I really liked her but there was this pressing issue that kept me from pursuing more. She had this living practice that baffled me. She lived in a house and she did not lock her doors at night or during the day while she was away. "Not locking your doors at home;" no way I thought. I came from the projects on the eastside of Detroit and the last thing you wanted to do was to leave your doors unlocked. The idea was too far-fetched; and it just didn't make common sense to me. My way of thinking ultimately pointed me in another direction. Even though I enjoyed the pleasant, positive and wonderful attitude she possessed, I just couldn't get over the unlocked doors, so I moved on.

During the process of getting to know Jean; I witnessed a different way of thinking about life and living life. It was refreshing and memorable. Not only did she afford me the opportunity to spend time around someone who had found a way to enjoy this experience we call life, but I learned a few things I could apply to my own life to enhance it. Jean introduced me to affirmations; these positive quotations and statements that were written down or you could create if you liked. So I began to write my own personal affirmations and used them as reminders for me to stay focused, especially when I would be around not so positive people. I remember one of my first personal affirmations was "Work, Play and Business equals time well spent." I had gotten into the habit of going dancing three to four nights a week and felt like I needed balance in my life. I needed to spend more time doing things that assisted me in growing, not just working and having fun. Work was work; play was fun, and business was anything that assisted me with my growth; be it reading a book, listening to a tape, gospel music, attending a lecture, taking a class, managing my money, my bills, etc. These were daily reminders to not get caught up in just working, dancing or having fun.

Since Jean, the most positive person I had met in years was no longer part of my life; I used affirmations to stay focused. *(Awareness, acceptance and active change)*

My positive minded life continued pretty much like that for a while, still without that girlfriend to complete it. Just as I had gotten a lift from the book "Your Erroneous Zones, and inspired by the gospel song "Be Grateful," I had gotten another boost, this time from affirmations. It was a different method but still aiming me in the direction I wanted to go.

The book and song had helped me see, be different and cope with my life better. I had continued to speak about my undesirable way of being in past tense, and reminded myself to be grateful for what I had instead of dwelling or focusing on what I did not have in my life at the time. However, when I stumbled upon the idea of using affirmations as a way of developing a positive attitude in place of having a negative one about life and people, I then had a third way of being that would allow me to live a fuller and happier life.

"Work, play and business equals time well spent," was placed all over the place. This particular affirmation seemed to keep me grounded in living a balanced life rather than working and playing or partying all the time.

I spent time reading more, and paid close attention to quotes that resonated with *the Best of Life* instead of spending time talking with friends and associates about people and things that revolved around *the Rest of Life*, or the less of life. Surrounding myself, with positive ideas until I could surround myself with positive people was my plan. It helped me change my focus, attitude, and my life reflected it. This endeavor supported my efforts to grow myself, make the changes I needed to evolve to the next level and was another example and benefit of seeking to find.

It was 1983; I was working at an airplane parts manufacturer; and got laid off from my job for the third time in three years. The two previous times, I was off for six months each time. This time if I was going to be off another six months I wanted to visit my mother, family and friends in Detroit. When, I made an inquiry I was informed I would not get a call back until around October, which would have been about six months later. With that in mind I headed back to Detroit. As it turned out, I was in Detroit for less than a week and was called back to work. I decided not to return and subsequently moved back to Detroit.

I am confident the book, the gospel song, introduction to affirmations along with my seek and ye shall find attitude, prepared me for my return to Detroit to meet positive people in a way I had not up until that point in my life.

In the upcoming chapter, I will talk about how my return was consistent with what I was seeking.

CHAPTER 3

I CHANGED MY PATH

I was at a point in time where I really wanted positive people to come into my life.

I had been, and still was willing to modify things about myself, if in doing so it would bring constructive change and people into my world. I asked for what I wanted; was willing to do the work to get it, and it was given. I accepted that a want without the work is just a wish.

My willingness to change my mind, myself and life, led to helpful and beneficial changes. After seeing and experiencing the benefits, I made a conscious effort to increase this practice. I changed the way I did things as well as the things I did.

I remained diligent about creating a more rewarding way of being, in doing so, more learning moments to increase my quality of life occurred.

I returned to Detroit; and the wonderful thing about returning was, the support I received for living a wonderful life, meeting pleasant and powerful people, and finding that recipe for happiness I was looking for. Within a year I got a job doing community service work again, working for the Detroit Urban League. At work I met Linda a wonderful co-worker who fit the description of a positive and pleasant person I had talked about while in San Diego. Surrounding myself with the affirmations put me on a path to actually meet and be comfortable around successful people who were living on that level. Not only was she positive, but through her I was able to meet other like-minded people. I was able to actually surround myself with people who were living peaceful, productive, and encouraging lives. I was not only introduced to people but also to a special kind of church. Unlike any other church I had been involved with growing up, it was different, and that something different had great appeal with me.

After returning home, not only did I make new acquaintances, in addition I was introduced to more eye opening ideas, programs, lectures, books, speakers and education. You name it and it appeared to be coming my way. By consistently making an effort to find that happiness recipe, it called me to seek, change my way of thinking and being. I was willing to make the changes.

Experiences were so different than they had been. I was glad about it. I had been alone with my affirmations in San Diego, but now I was being supported by real people, and not alone anymore.

I wanted to get others involved in my new experience of life. Nonetheless, just like my upbringing and beliefs about life prohibited me from accepting Jean's San Diego lifestyle, I felt I would meet resistance from my old friends with my new way of thinking.

I decided to continue with my new way of living, learn as much as I could, as fast as I could, which would allow me to better sell my "peeps" or people on my new found way to enjoy life. It was definitely on a different level than the one I had been exposed and accustomed to before I spent four years in college and five years in California.

Through my commitment to live a changed life, with new found friends, associates and a church, I was introduced to a host of events and enlightening experiences that supported my path toward that recipe for happiness I would one day call my own.

My pursuit of knowledge through education and experience continued. I looked for solutions and resolutions through others who had experienced the lifestyles which provided an alternative to the violence, abuse and dysfunction. I sought information that had been shared over the years that addressed the common problems we faced then and still collectively face today. I read the books, listened to recorded information, watched television programs, and pursued any forms of education that addressed the issues I wanted to see rectified. I engaged in daily practices and exercises that supported my personal development and allowed me to continue to grow and obtain my lifelong goal of finding a recipe for living a life full of joy, peace and happiness.

It's 1984, and I'm sitting in front of the television watching this early morning TV program, the Dynamic Achievers World Network, a program I had been introduced to by one of the intriguing people I had met through Linda, the wonderful co-worker of mine, at the Urban League.

It was brought to my attention that it was a worthwhile program to watch if I was interested in expanding my horizons. I looked into it and it was definitely worth my while.

To watch the Dynamic Achievers World Network program, I would wake up around 5:45am, so I could prepare and be ready by 6:00am to watch this half hour of personal power presented by some of the leading motivational and inspirational speakers in America. Not only did I watch the program, I would audiotape it as well. This would allow me to hear the half hour of inspiration over and over again until it became a part of my thinking and way of being. I was amazed how each program would provide something valuable to assist me in some way with my personal and, or spiritual growth. I had never seen such a television program before. I was still heavy into writing positive affirmations to help remind me of the living mindset I wanted for my life at the time.

On this particular morning the presenter spoke about the Terrible 10; or ten ways to kill success in your life. The ten ways to kill success caught my attention. I wrote them down on 3" x 5" cards, like I did with my positive affirmations over the years. I placed them on the mirror in my bathroom as well as on the side of the refrigerator. I used them as a constant visual reminder of the attitudes and characteristics that would get in the way of my success. I wanted to avoid them at all cost.

Take a look at them for yourself and see how they land on you, if they do.

The Terrible 10 that kill success:

1. Complaining
2. Criticizing
3. Fear of failure
4. Gossip
5. Greed
6. Indecision
7. Indifference
8. Pessimism
9. Procrastination
10. Worry

Allowing them to be a part of your being will interfere with success in your life. Eliminating these characteristics will increase your chance for success. I made a conscious effort to remove them from my life and in doing so kept myself on the path to living *the Best of Me*. Yes, the Terrible 10 represent *the Rest of You*, and definitely not *the Best of You*.

Detroit Unity Church was the local non-denominational that caught my attention in a big way. It was the church Linda was attending and the church where I got to meet people who seemed to be living the kind of life I was seeking for myself. It was definitely a welcomed change.

This non-denominational church had real church appeal. I was drawn to the fact I never heard conversation from members or ministers spending time or energy putting the practices and teachings of other churches down for not sharing the identical dogma, denomination or presentation of God. That was something I grew too familiar with in my experiences with previous churches. One church putting down another church, another denomination, had seemed to be a large part of the themes which ran through community churches I had attended.

This church welcomed the dialogue and sharing of the teaching and experiences people of different faiths, backgrounds and denominations had experienced. Regardless of who they were, they acknowledged a Higher Power; God, Creator, a unified expression of love throughout the world.

At this church I wasn't hearing about how their way was the only way. Time was spent embracing one another's experience of God, Lord, Jesus Christ or whatever the name one may have used to depict his or her Creator, Deliverer or King of Kings. The church welcomed people of different races, creeds and colors, as well as the philosophies of various. For the first time in 10 years I began attending church regularly.

I found people, places and practices which resonated with my longing for answers and for the elimination of the violence, abuse and dysfunction I had been exposed to growing up. To me this new church represented peace, joy, advancement and happiness for all; a message I had been seeking.

I remember listening to Ted Hunt, a motivational speaker from the Detroit area, speak to a group of children at one of the schools where I worked. Something he said seemed so simple to do, and at the same time could make such an impact on others. He asked for the students to make a point to find at least one thing nice to say about anyone or everyone they met. He said we could find something nice to say about anyone if we just took the time to look for it; and just a simple gesture as that could make all the difference in the world for someone who might be hurting on the inside but camouflaging it on the outside. "A kind word can go a long way" he expressed.

I took on the practice and found that it was not only something nice to do but gratifying to do as well. That concept as well as another one that says, "If you don't have anything nice to say, don't say anything at all." I felt they complimented one another, and resonated with me. They both are definitely aspects of living *the Best of You*.

Mr. Hunt was also a guest speaker at Detroit Unity. I heard "Birds of a feather flock together," and I believe positive people share positive ideas and insight.

My life was working so well I thought I was getting close to my recipe, and found myself wanting to share what I had learned with others. I asked for what I wanted, was willing to do the work to get it, and it was given. It represented me continuing to be diligent about creating a different way of being in a different lifestyle than what I had been accustomed. My commitment and diligence enabled me to find more people, books, lectures, tapes, and programs, you name it, which would support me in developing qualities representative of *the Best of Me.*

I had been gathering insightful information over a period of a few years, and decided to begin using my artistic drawing ability to take my affirmations, and create pictures to go with them to make posters that I could sell. I wanted to create some kind of business around a lifestyle which had become such a part of me. My new business venture led me to an encounter with a young lady name Bettie Barton. Through our chance meeting, my definition of the way I saw competition and ultimately myself, changed. Meeting her at that print shop that day, was the day the path I was on began changing me in the biggest and best of ways.

My life after that chance meeting is revealed in the upcoming chapter. The difference a day can make.

CHAPTER 4

THE PATH CHANGED ME

A real shift had taken place in my life. The people, places and principles were coming and working wonders for me. For quite a while I had made it a point to change my ways, if doing so would increase my quality of life, my understanding about how to live, and get me closer to finding the recipe for happiness I had been searching for.

It appeared as if I was being supported in my new way of being. The way I had been living was like swimming upstream, making life hard on myself. I came to find that what I needed was to turn around and swim downstream, to allow the natural flow of the Universe like the water to assist in my effort and experiences. I realized that in my less than *Best* old way of being, I was going against natural laws and living principles. With a new way of looking at life and re-defining myself, my living experience was being supported by an unfamiliar source of assistance.

I chose a different path to find a better way. The more I searched the more I found. The more I found the more I was convinced this way was real. Support was coming to and through me effortlessly. I found myself not needing to go out and make things happen, but instead staying the course of my new found Truth and watched as support arrived. I was involved in a totally different existence, a wonderful experience of life, with a lot less effort exerted than when I was on my former living path.

It was the Spring of 1984 I had a chance meeting with Bettie Barton, a highly regarded school teacher in the Detroit Public School system, at a graphic print shop on the west side of Detroit. The way she carried herself and the display of unsolicited help and support to those who were around her was surprising to me. She was a patron just like I was, however, the way she so openly offered help and assistance while we waited in line peaked curiosity in me.

There was something about her that led me to believe she had, and knew something I didn't that could help me with my quest to find that recipe for happiness.

After my quick pursuit to find out more about her, she invited me to a class she was teaching at a local church. That church just happened to be the same church my co-worker had introduced me to, where I had met so many positive and powerful people since returning to Detroit. I accepted her offer and became a student in her weekly class. New ways of being *the Best of Me* was expanding in my life, go figure.

Bettie was the closest person to exemplify the personality, the way of being I was looking for in people. I saw her as the model person for how one could live a life of joy, peace and happiness without the traditional emphasis on money.

The thought of me being mentored by her was an unbelievable and welcomed experience that truly changed me in the biggest way. Not only did she continue to add to the wonderful life I had been exposed to, but took it to another level. Her one-on-one coaching and support brought about the most profound change in my life. She helped me to establish a new definition of *Self*, and how it applied to me, exposing me to a new way of living.

It became apparent later, that the day we met in the print shop was the day the path I was on began changing me in the biggest and best of ways. It laid the foundation for a wonderful and enjoyable life ahead.

Bettie Barton was a God send, she changed my life forever. Prior to her coming into my life it was a book, song, written affirmations and positive people whom I learned lessons from. As a result, I was moving away from the violence, abuse, dysfunction and problems that I had been attached to for so long. I was moving away from them and I loved it. Bettie brought something that had not been shared before; she brought a mindset, a way of thinking and being that not only changed me, but transformed my way of life. You might say how and why is that? It's because of what we talked about, and what she shared that went straight to the core of me.

From my time spent talking and sharing with Bettie I realized the first thing I needed to do in any relationship, be it personal, private, or public was to define and remember who I am.

We talked about, "What is life? What is living? Who are we? Why we're here?" Our conversations about, "Who I am went further than my name, title, or position. For years if someone asked me who I was, my typical response was "I'm Melvin Foreman." However she elevated my level of thinking. She helped me realize if we were going to solve the problems, issues and concerns in our lives, we needed to re-establish the definition of ourselves at a higher level than what we had been operating on or from. Whatever description, label, or level I had created, accepted or was seeing myself at, would be where I would live from, and my experience of life would reflect that.

She helped me to understand, that the definition of myself in which I lived would determine my experience of life. With that awareness, or introduction to that awareness, caused me to think about it. If I saw myself only as my name then I would live from anything and everything I had done because anything and everything that I had done was who Melvin Foreman was. If I saw myself as the good yet shy twin then anything and everything that I did would come from that space. I realized that had been my experience until I accepted this new definition for myself. My definition of *Self* worked when supporting *the Rest of Me* and could work now just on a different level, supporting *the Best of Me*.

From my conversations with her, I was hearing that if I lived my life from my highest level of being, I could do and experience things that I had not done or experienced before. I could behave, see and be in a way I had not been before. What needed to be done was to see myself at the highest level of *Self*. In doing so, I would be able to transcend the behavior, thoughts, and labels I had been given, and those I had given others which predicated the way in which we related. This was an opportunity for me to see and live my life differently.

I began to define myself as a *Kingdom Kid*, child of God; here on Earth to share and support love. It changed how I saw myself and how I would continue my journey through life. I was a *Kingdom Kid*, and through Bettie and her seemingly daily support, the learning moments, life lessons, growth and love expanded.

One of the biggest impacts outside of my new found definition of myself was this view that life is either *Love or Lesson*. Collectively, we have been stuck in the lesson phase of our experiences, but not learning from them. At any time in life that you are not feeling loving about something or someone, there is a lesson to learn. The key and what's most important is that you make time to ask, "What can I learn from this, so I can return from this to *Love?*" You know you have learned the lesson when you can see whatever you felt less than loving about differently, and be at peace with it. If you are not at peace with it, you have not learned your true lesson. This applies individually and collectively. It may not be the easiest thing to do initially, especially when you're trying to apply this practice with what you would consider major issues in your life. Therefore, if you are having difficulty with it, utilize it with smaller challenges, and get some answers under your belt. As you practice, your answers and strength will increase. As you get stronger you will be able to handle heavier, larger, and more tasks with greater ease.

Bettie was a teacher in the Detroit Public School system, and just being around her, listening to her life story inspired me to consider going into teaching myself. I sought employment as an emergency substitute teacher to get my feet wet, while I contemplated whether teaching in school was something I wanted to do. I knew at the time I didn't want to go into debt with student loans if more education was going to be required and I knew to some degree it would. I hoped that maybe, just maybe, I would find some type of program that would pay for my education to return to school to get a teaching certification. If an opportunity presented itself, that would help me decide. In the meantime, I would simply work as a substitute teacher to get a feel for what it could be like teaching in Detroit.

For the next two years during every substitute teaching assignment, I viewed and carried myself first and foremost as a *Kingdom Kid*, there to share and support love. I saw my second responsibility as a substitute teacher to assist the students in whatever subject matter I was covering that day. This approach provided me with the most wonderful experiences; in a position so many had suggested would not be pleasant because of the mindset, "when the teacher's away the students will play." It was an unbelievable two years of living a life filled with more joy, peace and happiness.

I knew if it had not been for Bettie and her insight shared, I would not have had such a wonderful time working as a substitute teacher. She was the living model, teacher and student of the truth I was seeking. The Bettie I came to know was the person I was looking for when I pursued her; she represented a living persona which I had only imagined one could be like. She helped lay a strong foundation and a daily practice that ultimately led me to the happiness recipe I was searching for in life.

Bettie had an all-in now approach to get desired results, while I preferred a gradual approach to the end. Based on where she was on her journey and where I was at the time; our levels and some views differed. We both had a burning desire to live a life of love, joy, peace and happiness; however, Bettie knew how, while I sought to learn.

- Bettie and I believed the state of violence, abuse and dysfunction was not the way it had to be.
- We both were interested in living a life of love and joy.
- We both looked for ways not only to improve the quality of our lives but the lives of others.
- We both used our artistic abilities to create visuals, to share with others in efforts to support their and our enrichment experience.
- We both saw ourselves as students and teachers. We both worked as professional teachers.

I wanted to be a good student and learn; she was a model student of truth which had the foundation and ingredients I was seeking in life. My eagerness to learn allowed me the opportunity to get to know Bettie, as well as her way of thinking. I found her way of thinking and being to be intriguing and helpful; however, I did not feel I was ready for the higher level coaching and exercises she encouraged me to take on.

Regardless of the challenges of our differences, I openly and wholeheartedly welcomed her, the person and the mentor into my world, life and thinking. I saw her then as God sent and continue to see her that way today.

When the time came and it was apparent that I wanted to precede going forward in a slightly different manner, she allowed and accepted where I was, as she stood steadfast in her practice. She wasn't trying to change me; nor was she going to be swayed from her way of being. The wonderful committed woman she was to her practice of Truth when we met, she continued to be. We had studied faithfully daily; until the time came when we parted ways.

She had been a student of the book "A Course in Miracles"; and it was the strongest source of spiritual insight over the course of my study time with her. Our time spent together laid the foundation for a transformed personal life and ultimately the foundation which led to my ultimate recipe for happiness, or *Best Self Living* which will be covered in a later chapter in the book.

I slowly slipped away from the daily interactions with my mentor; but I took with me a changed way of being which continued to shine and work for me and my life, in ways I had hoped for but never really imagined. My world and experiences were changing. I was in awe of what was happening and the reality of this new way of being. I had adopted the *Love or Lesson* practice for some years when I found myself faced with one of my biggest challenges in putting this practice to use. We live in a racially divided country and society. Even though I had wonderful interracial experiences along with practicing the Living Principle of One Love, I still recognized that I was not fully immune to allowing common practice or common ways of thinking to seep into my thought process and way of being.

On this particular afternoon, I was on my way to work and had made a left turn onto a major street in Detroit. Within a few blocks of making that turn, I was pulled over by a white police officer. I don't recall what had been present in the news around black and white problems or issues in the city at that time, but I do remember being highly upset for being stopped by this white police officer. He said he pulled me over because I had made an illegal turn. I however, believed he pulled me over and gave me a ticket not because of the turn I made, which I feverously denied was illegal; not because I did not have proof of insurance on me; not because the outside mirror on the driver side of my car was missing, but because I was black and he was white. After receiving my ticket I proceeded to work and began my *Love or Lesson* ritual. "Lord I am not feeling real loving right now, what can I learn from this so I can return from this to love." Again, "Lord I am not feeling real loving right now what can I learn from this so I can return from this to love." I continued to repeat that prayer ritual on my way to work, while I was at work and on my way home afterwards. For some reason or another, I could not seem to find peace with what had happened that day with that police officer. I found myself going back and forth between "what can I learn from this and if that white officer gave me a ticket because I was a black man?" This challenge and back-and-forth process went on for about two or three weeks and I just could not seem to find peace with it. It wasn't until the day I went to court to fight the ticket that my answer came. I had three things to do according to the police officer:

1)   Show up in court if I wanted to fight the ticket.

2) Bring proof of auto insurance to court (I could not find it the day he gave me the ticket).

3) Show proof of having my outside mirror replaced.

I got my outside mirror replaced, I had proof of insurance and I showed up to court to fight the ticket. I went before the judge I showed proof of both the mirror repair and insurance and because the officer didn't show up my ticket was thrown out. "Hip, hip, hooray," no ticket, no fine, and no points on my record; which meant no increase in my auto insurance rate.

I left court a happy camper but still had not figured out what my lesson was. Wouldn't you know it, a few hours later my answer came? I was able to see the officer and the situation with the ticket differently. I realized that I had been driving my car without that left outside mirror for quite some time. A couple of times I had close calls with cars on the freeway speeding pass me on my left side at high rates of speed around the same time I was planning on moving to my left. I had ignored these occurrences and continued driving regardless; too busy to replace that left outside mirror. What was it going to take for me to make time to replace that mirror? Little did I know, rather than making the entire experience about me being black and the police officer being white, I was able to see at a higher level it could be the difference in me having the experience of a safe drive during my daily commutes or continually setting myself up for what could lead to a terrible if not fatal accident. I had become too busy going to and fro to stop and make a short simple necessary repair to my car for my own driving well-being. It took my experience with the officer and the illegal turn accusation for me to get started handling my much needed business. "Bingo," there was my answer. Thank you for my unknowing support.

For me it was proof once again life is either *Love or Lesson*. I realized if I truly want to live a life of love I would have to practice that principle wherever I go and whatever I do, regardless of whom the experience may involve. I believe the principle is so powerful that even if others themselves are not living their purpose in love and are trying to do you injustice, ill will, or even harm; if you stick to the principle and apply it you will get the same true lesson and the blessing that comes from learning the lesson. We are here to expand our capacity to love. (*Awareness, acceptance and change*)

Even with my curiosity and pursuit of an alternative way of living, the influence of my cultural upbringing and community experiences still played a part in my basic belief about life and the way things are.
My hope and dream of finding a recipe for happiness represented my pursuit of a changed way of living. My strong ambition to find a new way of experiencing life required a personal change in my views and thinking.

I was not aware of what changes needed to be made at the onset of my journey, but I accepted them, based on the information I gathered, and the people I met along the way. I got to understand from the individuals who lived, taught and supported the kind of happy living I wanted.

I came to realize that in order for the type of change that I was looking for to happen, transformation needed to take place beginning with me. I learned that change on a small scale was like moving the position of chairs in a room; however the magnitude of change I was looking for would require change more like moving from one mode of transportation to another; living from one level of thinking to another. I accepted that the problems I was attempting to solve could not be solved looking at them from the same level they were created on, but needed to be viewed from a higher level of thinking. It was like the difference between adding and subtraction and using multiplication.

At the onset of my journey I believed to a large extent that it was the people out there who were the cause of my individual headaches and heartaches. I believed that it was those folks that dictated the experience of life I would have. I had been led to believe that I and the people around me were victims of circumstances; the "it's like that, and that's the way it is" mentality had validity.

However, in pursuit of an alternative way or living a better life, I gained a different understanding of the big picture, which caused my view to change.

Over the course of my journey I shifted my way of seeing life and the experiences of people in it. I moved from living or looking at life from the outside in to living my life from the inside out.

I moved from living life based on up and down feelings, symptoms of fear like anger, hatred, jealousy and guilt; to a life based on who I am at my highest level of expression.

My life experiences were profoundly transforming me. I was exposed to ways of being that answered questions I had about what to do; which provided me insight into lovingly living a life I love. *(Awareness, Acceptance, and Active Change)*

In the next chapter I will share how this helped transform my life.

CHAPTER 5

THE PATH THAT KEEPS ON GIVING

My quality of life was transforming. It seemed as if my commitment to be different in my thinking and approach to life was paying off in a big way, one event after another. My life was unlike than it had been; the longer I worked with and practiced the Principles, the more success I had getting results from living that way.

Declaring and living from my new definition of *Self*, combined with doing what I love to do provided a mindset, energy and new vitality to my work and life experience. I worked with a confidence that said whatever I was doing it would turn out well because of who I was, whose I was, and what I was doing. The *Universe* had my back; I was being and living well.

I saw things differently, the experiences changed my view and the training paid off. Bettie Barton's mentorship had transformed me. I continued to practice and pursue both personally and culturally my happiness recipe. As I continued, so did my success.

Life was good but I still had not settled on what my career path would be. In my lifetime I had worked a few jobs but still couldn't decide on what I wanted to do for the next 20 or 30 years. *(Lost and seeking)*

I continued to study and practice. I then heard about an upcoming workshop that would be held at the church, said to be awesome, entitled "You Can Have it All" a money mastery program by Arnold Patent. I couldn't wait; the idea of more money sounded great especially after how disappointing it had been making the kind of money I had made since graduating from college with a Bachelor of Arts degree. I had been led to believe that with a college degree I would automatically be able to get a good paying job, but in my case that was not a reality. I was upset at the fact that some of the guys I had grown up with in the projects were making more money working for one of the big 3 auto makers in Detroit right out of high school than I was after graduating with a degree. This had been my experience for seven years; by that time in my life I was ready to master money.

I went into the workshop unsure of a career path; and came out of the experience able to pursue a career doing what I truly loved to do. The area I chose was a profession where I had made a mere $5 per hour working and had no idea how I could make a living in that field. However, a key principle that resonated with me was the one that said "Doing what you truly love to do" is a basic *Universal Principle*. I was reminded that we are all created with a purpose and doing what you truly love to do aligns you with your Purpose. It has nothing to do with money, power or position; it is strictly based upon doing what you truly love to do and having *Universal* support. The *Universe* was created perfectly and living our Purpose is part of that perfection. *(Awareness)*

During the "You Can Have It All" workshop, I realized just how many of us said we didn't know what we truly loved to do, or had so many choices that made it difficult to decide. Arnold, the facilitator brought up the idea that all of the indecision was nothing more than a classic case of avoidance. It all represented a fear of getting on with a wonderful life, and trusting that the *Universe* was set up perfectly to support us. Just hearing that, I wasn't sold on it. However, when the idea of owning the level was presented, I was more willing to take a leap of faith. Owning the level suggested that picking one thing that you love to do out of the many and getting 100% behind it would not be a waste of time. After picking one, if it came to a point where you realize that particular choice was not the one, you could choose another. In doing so you would not have to start from ground zero because whatever level of success you had with the previous choice would transfer to your new one. The idea of not starting over from square one sat well with me. I was able to choose teaching tennis as the thing I loved to do. Immediately, after doing so, I shared my love for teaching tennis with workshop participants and got 15 people to sign up for a tennis program I would put together. *(Acceptance)*

The "You Can Have it All" book and workshop played a large part in my life change. My broad interpretation from both combined with my life experiences brought me to suggest that:

- You want to be mindful of the definitions you accept for yourself because the definitions you embrace help determine your experience of life.

- We all can look at the same thing and give different definitions of what it is or what it means to us. Make sure the meanings that you give to life, serve your greater good, the greater good of others and life in general.

- That which you accept, believe, and promote you support. If you don't want violence, abuse and dysfunction around don't support it.

Give time and energy to that in which you want and eliminate energy and effort for that you do not desire.

The workshop changed my life. In the spring of 1985, I started Twin Tennistry, a tennis business. I taught an adult tennis program at Peterson Park on the west side of Detroit, and coached youth aged 7-17 for the city of Detroit Police Athletic League/Parks & Recreation Summer Junior Tennis program at Clark Park. It was my first year doing so and I was awarded Outstanding Tennis Coach of the Year. I also expanded my adult tennis program to the eastside of Detroit in July of that year. I bought into the "do what you truly love to do" mindset and was moving ahead with my life like that was how it was supposed to be lived. *(Active practice)*

I was involved in my passion (teaching tennis) as well as working and having success as an emergency substitute teacher. I was on an

unbelievable roll and didn't want it to end.

I was at a point where my life had taken such a wonderful turn, leading me to accept new definitions for my future to live by. A different kind of life than the one I had while living in San Diego had emerged. I had come from "Being Grateful" yet not truly happy, from surrounding myself with positive affirmations to surrounding myself with positive people. They exposed me to ways of living and ways of being that set me on a path that provided me with a life I had once only dreamed of. *(Attainment)*

Who am I, why am I here? A *Kingdom Kid*, a child of God, here to share and support love was my living definition of *Self*. Now I was being introduced to doing what I truly loved to do as another living principle. *(Awareness)*

I came to understand that so often people are working on jobs or in careers that have nothing to do with what they love, but instead

MELVIN D. FOREMAN

are merely motivated by money. Led by how much money and position power they could obtain with no emphasis on doing what they truly love and were created to do. Are you living like this instead of doing what you have a passion for and allowing the money to follow?

Abundance is the natural state of the *Universe*, and if you are not experiencing abundance in your life it is only because you are actively keeping it away. This philosophy challenges the common mindset that if you want something you have to work hard for it, and if you want to be successful, you have to have a lot of money. I accepted that money is the byproduct of living your passion and you need not go after money to get what you want. When you go after your passion or live from your passion, whatever it is that you want is there before the money, when you have the money, and after the money if for some reason it leaves you.

I moved to living life based on who I am at the highest level of expression, a *Kingdom Kid*, child of God. I accepted that I am here to live my purpose, share and support *Love*, and do what I truly love to do.

I also accepted that life was either *Love or Lesson*; and seeing it accordingly was the way to move through it peacefully and successfully. I was convinced we are all meant to grow mentally, emotionally, spiritually, socially, physically, professionally and financially; with the spiritual aspect carrying the utmost importance. *(Awareness, Acceptance and Active Change)*

54

I moved from living life according to the past, pain, pitfalls and problems to living from purpose, passion, power and peace. I shifted from living life based on possessions and doing, to living a life based on Being, the essence of who I am.

Throughout the course of my life I had vacillated back and forth between my old way of thinking and being, and my new found way of living a life I loved. I ultimately rest my laurels on living the principles of *the Best of Me* rather than the practices of *the Rest of Me*.

It's the mid 1980's, my life was working wonderfully but not without incident.

Many of my associates at the time would discuss with me issues and problems they were having in their lives. I openly and willingly would share my living philosophy and how it was working so wonderfully well in my life. However, over a period of time, I began to realize that a common response from my associates was "It's easy for you to be positive, and talk about how wonderful life is when you are not experiencing the problems that I'm experiencing in my life." Little did I know, according to living principles, me trying to convince others is not necessary, nor a wise thing to do. What's most important is to share and support love while encouraging others to do the same. There's no need for shoving what's so for me down their throats or trying to convince them of anything. Everything is in Divine Order for those who believe. With that being said, if you have friends not believing as you do it still qualifies as being in Divine Order. I came to believe that there is nothing wrong with others seeing themselves where they are. However, in the mid 1980's I had not grown to that level of understanding, and therefore consistently and persistently tried to convince my friends, associates, or others to see life the way I was seeing it. I later came to understand that, trying to get others to see life as I see it, when I see it is a way of trying to control them.

My car was broken into. The car radio and some audiotapes were stolen, and I shrugged it off. I kept honoring the *Universal Principles* I had accepted to live by. "Look what I created and attracted, it's in *Divine Order*" I suggested. My response didn't impress my associates enough to buy into what I was saying about how wonderful life could be living according to the *Principles* I was enjoying.

In my mind there had to be some way for me to get them to believe what I was sharing as truth. I was determined to show as well as convince them that these *Principles* were real, had validity and worked; and then it happened.

On this particular Sunday afternoon, I stopped at a payphone on the west side of Detroit. Yes, it was 1987, before the cellular phone era, when phone booths existed, and you could stand outside and make a 25 cents unlimited local call. I had been on the phone for no more than 5 minutes when I was approached by a young man who claimed to have a gun, and requested that I give him my money. I did not realize at first what was going on, but soon realized I was about to be robbed in broad daylight on a Sunday, a few hours after attending church.

Can you imagine what I felt when I realized He who created me, the Heavens and the Earth had wrapped His loving arms around me as I looked down the barrel of a loaded handgun six inches from my face?

Later that day, I pulled to the side of the road and cried real tears. Only an hour before I fought with a guy where my life could have been taken in an instant. If that trigger had been pulled, another wonderful life could have ended. After I had wrestled the gun away from the perpetrator, some passer byers helped hold him down until the police arrived; my life had been spared.

Oh what a blessing. A sad and wonderful event had intertwined that Sunday afternoon. After all was said and done, I realized God loved me, and had wrapped his arms around me that day to let me know. He held me long enough and in such a way that I resisted the strong urge to shoot the guy after wrestling the gun away from him.

With all the fear and anger running through my mind and body at the time, I could have committed an unthinkable act myself.

I thank God I didn't.

I believe I was given notice of God's love not just for me, but for us all. I believe His will is for us to remember who He is, and his provision of unconditional, unified love for us to live while we are here.

I could have died or gone to prison based on the events that took place that day but I was spared. I was still allowed to go forth to live, love, learn and grow. I am forever grateful.

After pulling off on the side of the road and having a good cry, I was still committed to the insight I had gained and looked forward to continued practice. I began like I had done so many times before when I had an experience of less than loving feelings about something or someone; I asked "Lord, what can I learn from this, so I can return from this to love?" I definitely wasn't feeling loving about the most frightening experience I had just gone through. I kept repeating it over and over periodically throughout the days that followed, in between telling family and friends about the unexpected heart pounding ordeal. Ultimately when the answer came, it came like most of them would come; when I wasn't consciously looking for it. It was usually when I was in a calm state of mind, after I had asked and just let it be.

It is so important to quit looking to prove to others what you have come to know for yourself. This revelation came to me after an

58

extreme situation or circumstance, but it is not your job to try and force truth as you know it down other people's throat. Just like you got it when you were ready, they will get it when they are as well. It will happen when they are ready. All you have to do is continue to share and support love and be the example. When those who seek to know come, and they will; you can then share your experience in love.

I came to realize I had been making it more about me and what I knew, than about sharing love and support. The whole experience was one of the most heartfelt life changing lessons. I promised myself and God that my days of trying to make people see what I was seeing, the way I was seeing it, were over. I realized that I was no longer willing, nor ready to force my understanding on anyone. It is not necessary and it goes against the natural laws or *Universal Principles*. I accepted the fact it is more about me sharing the food (insight) I have acquired, not shoving it down the throat of others.

My life had become a successful one in my eyes and I was now grateful on a whole different level. I still wasn't making a significant amount of money teaching tennis, however, I was doing what I love to do and the response I had gotten up until that point was positive and looked promising. I stayed tuned into the love of it, the support I was getting, and looked forward to the financial reward coming.

A year earlier in the summer of 1986, while attending a lecture, I adopted a working philosophy I picked up from motivational speaker Les Brown. He said something to the affect, "Work full time on your job and part-time on your fortune or what you love to do until the day comes when you can give up that job to do what you love full time."

That led me to accept a job sewing seat covers at Chrysler Corporation at the time making three to four times the amount of money I had been making teaching tennis. The plan was to work full time at Chrysler and part time doing what I loved, which was teaching tennis until I found a way to make more than $5 an hour doing so.

It had been two years since my shift to living my new definition of *Self*, doing what I truly loved to do, and a year since I worked as an emergency substitute teacher.

Richard Jackson, a local avid tennis player who I had met while teaching and playing tennis a couple years earlier took it upon himself to contact me about a tennis opportunity as a coach with Arthur Ashe & Nick Bollettieri at the world famous Nick Bollettieri Tennis Academy in Bradenton, Florida. Richard told me he had watched me teach and felt I would be an excellent candidate for this tennis opportunity for coaches he had heard about on the radio.

At that particular time, based on my experience, I did not know how I could make a decent living teaching tennis. I had come to believe you were either a playing professional like Arthur Ashe or Jimmy Connors or a tennis enthusiast who played at a local park. I felt making a living outside of playing wasn't a working career path, especially in the inner city.

However, I continued believing in the principles from the "You Can Have it All" workshop and the experience I was having as a *Kingdom Kid* even though sometimes wavered in my trust that the *Universe* supported me.

The unexpected call from Richard Jackson telling me about the internship program for tennis coaches Arthur Ashe and Nick Bollettieri was putting together simply reinforced my belief.

I pursued the opportunity. I was accepted into the six month internship program which cost $6,000, and awarded a $4,000 scholarship to attend. The success I was having on my journey toward finding a living recipe of happiness while trusting a source of supply greater than me continued.

Not only did I attend the internship program, but within a year's time, I went from earning $5 an hour teaching tennis in Detroit to a $60,000 a year tennis job working for the first Arthur Ashe/Nick Bollettieri Inner City Tennis Program in Newark, New Jersey.

I was living a dream using a living philosophy I had only heard of some three years before. Being a *Kingdom Kid*, Child of God, and doing what I truly loved to do had gotten my attention in the biggest way.

I was the same guy who finished college ten years earlier with a college degree in Sociology and a mere $10,000 a year job upon graduation. My new adopted philosophy and way of living seemed to be working out. I was sold on the idea of living my life based on *Universal Principles* versus the generational and cultural practices I grew up hearing and witnessing.

The success with the new awareness, acceptance and change that had taken place in my life was overwhelming; however, it was a welcomed feeling of disbelief. I continued to run with it with a way of being unlike any I had been exposed to growing up on the eastside of Detroit.

The job position I accepted with the Ashe/Bollettieri tennis program in Newark was as the city tennis coordinator. The jump in the amount of money I was making compared to the year before was unbelievable and wonderful.

Conversely, a key premise shared in the "You Can Have it All" workshop that had me step out on faith in the first place was the concept of doing what you truly love to do, not doing what you do because of position power, prestige or money. I came to understand that if you did what you truly love to do the *Universe* would support you and the money would follow. Well, I chose tennis and within a year the money had followed. *(Awareness)*

After some deep thought and consideration I decided that the position I was holding as the city tennis coordinator was not what I truly loved to do and therefore was willing to step down to work as a tennis instructor for the program. In doing so, I would be taking a $40,000 a year pay cut. I shared the news with the National Director, and he couldn't believe his ears, but ultimately told me he would investigate the possibility. He would be out of town for a couple of weeks and would share his decision when he returned. (Acceptance)

While he was gone I returned home to visit my family. After returning to Detroit, I volunteered for a Detroit Recreation Department (DRD) Saturday night tennis event. I found out later the event was the kickoff for a city-wide tennis program. The program mirrored the proposal I had left with the executive secretary when I was declined the position of Tennis Coordinator some six months earlier. The person who had become the Tennis coordinator for the city of Detroit was present; after observing my work that night we scheduled an appointment for the upcoming week where he offered me a job as his tennis assistant. I accepted, and that was the start of my tennis career with the City of Detroit which spanned some 25 plus years. *(Change)*

I was offered a job to teach tennis half the amount of time per week making the same $20,000 I would have if I had stayed in

Newark working as one of the program instructors.

My journey had taken me from $5 an hour to $60,000 per year and back to a $20,000 (20 hours per week) contract, living back home with family. The way things were happening in my life said to me that this way of living, based on *Universal Principles*, was working and I was overjoyed. Not only was I going to make the same amount of money I was willing to work for in Newark, but I would work half the hours back home in Detroit. To be back with family and loved ones was a dream come true.

In an indirect way I unknowingly planted the seed for an upstart initiative tennis program in which I would ultimately come back to the city and run some six or so months later. Often I wondered what if I had not left my tennis proposal when I did. There is a strong possibility I would have never been given the opportunity to volunteer that unexpected Saturday night, which led to my 25 plus years of service with the DRD. The DRD Director may have rejected me as the tennis coordinator earlier in the year. However, by leaving my proposal and program ideas when I was turned down allowed me to return as the assistant to the coordinator and implement my proposed ideas anyway.

This new position I was offered in my mind was the *Universe* supporting me in living *the Best of Me*.

In addition to how amazing my return home experience had been, something else fascinated me. Five or six years earlier while working in a factory in San Diego California, I came up with a bright idea. I thought about how nice it would be to have a job where I

64

worked six months on, and six months off. This idea came about while working in a particular factory for a year or so, where I was laid off for six months, recalled back to work and then within a year laid off again. As an adult I had always done a good job managing my money and therefore my six months off from work was never a strain but more so like a vacation from work. I believe this is what led me to the idea of working six months on and six months off. In truth it was a radical or strange idea at the time, but one I thought would be nice if it was at all possible.

It was five or six years later but, receiving a yearly work contract with the Detroit Recreation Department for 20 hours a week was the equivalent of me working six months on and six months off at a traditional 40 hour a week salary.

I was not only astonished at how all of this had come about, but also how an underlining wish or desire could manifest itself concurrently with doing what I truly loved to do. *(Awareness and Acceptance)*

Stars seem to have aligned; and I was enjoying life.

a.   I was doing what I loved to do professionally.

b.   I was working the proposal I had left when originally denied the job opportunity.

c.   I was working the equivalent of six months on and six months off.

d.   My current supervisor appreciated me and my work. I was able to get everything I needed from the director who wouldn't hire me months earlier.

These experiences unfolded like previous events had in my life. Without a doubt, I was sold on the living Principles I had accepted as my own.

During this time I met and married one of my former tennis students. When I married her I did not know that I was marrying a financially independent woman. I had my money, she had her money, (which was significantly more); so we had our individual bank accounts and a joint account that we used to pay household bills and upkeep. It was a blessing that allowed me to continue doing what I loved to do, teach tennis in Detroit.

Working for the Detroit Recreation Department as tennis director was not financially lucrative but it was serving me just fine. As a result of not having to concern myself with day-to-day financial burdens, I was free to focus and concentrate on doing what I truly loved to do without concerning myself with money.

The real blessing is how this manifested like so many other gifts of support had over the course of my life. I was able to continue living without the conscious effort or pressure to make things happen; a philosophy we hear frequently in our traditional cultural way of thinking; "If you want something to happen, you have to go out and make it happen." Definitely not the life changing philosophy I had adopted which says "Abundance is the natural state of the *Universe*; get in touch with doing what you truly love to do, and the

Universe will support you and handle the details." So you might ask; why did I bring this up at this time? Well, not only was I able to maintain living a happily married life with new responsibilities but without the financial concerns. She also was someone who provided me with balance, and insight into other important aspects that had been missing in my life.

In addition, for years I thought I did not want to marry someone with a large family; an attitude that had developed based on my relationships with my small family of four. Although we loved one another we pretty much lived four separate lives. The adult family dinners, family gatherings, day in and day out conversations were not a typical part of my wonderful *Best of Me* living experience. I had lived most of my adult life doing what I loved to do, enjoying the benefits of doing that while at the same time accepting that I loved my family but we didn't see eye-to-eye enough to do those family kinds of things on a day-to-day basis. Given the issues that I had experienced and held onto involving my family dynamics, the last thing I wanted to do was marry someone with a large family.

My wife's relationship with her family showed me how a different experience of family could be. A truer blessing could not have been brought to me.

Was the *Universe* supporting me and rewarding me for sharing love and supporting love doing what I truly loved to do? I think so. Watching and observing her and the relationships between her and her mother, sisters, brothers, and extended family opened my eyes to a new world and definition of family.

The apprehension I had over the years about marrying into a large family was shown to be just that and nothing more.

Being married to my wife allowed me to attend family functions on a regular basis; celebrate holidays with family; plan, prepare for picnics and family trips. Her family getting together for a fish fry on any given day was not out of the question. Her family gathering for no other reason than to just get together seemed to be their modus operandi. Meaningful family fun gatherings I use to have with my own family happened primarily when we were kids; as an adult it was something we did rarely. How wonderful it was to have another unexpected part of my life redefined in *the Best of ways.*

I marveled at the experiences and increased supply in my life. I enjoyed a new life as more experiences that supported my new way of being came, and one gift seemed to lead to another.

a.   Arnold Patents book "You Can Have it All."

b.   My tennis, work attitude, Richard Jackson phone call.

c.   Working for Arthur Ashe and Nick Bollettieri.

d.   Witnessing my earning go from $5 an hour to $60,000 a year within a year.

e.   The Detroit Recreation Department not hiring me as coordinator; me leaving my proposed idea only to return some months later to actually implement the tennis proposal I had left.

I continued to stay the course. As long as I remained on the path the blessings continued to come. I was truly living my life from a different view. The *Universe* was supporting me in doing what I truly loved to do and one wonderful powerful thing led to another. Blessings would show up and come to me effortlessly. I marveled in this new experience, I marveled in this new way of living based on my way of being.

Along with numerous tennis and leadership positions, contracts, and awards; I continued my lifelong learner education through organizations and courses such as Toastmasters, Dale Carnegie, Stephen Covey's First Things First, Seven Habits of Highly Effective People, just to name a few. I was living much of my life as *the Best of Me* but still some parts as *the Rest of Me*, holding on to the right and wrong of things.

I will share more about this in the upcoming chapter; how it impacted me and what became of it in the scheme of things.

CHAPTER 6

CHOOSE TO CHOOSE AGAIN

Life is an ongoing process, more lessons to learn and hurdles to clear. When you feel stuck in a rut, and things don't seem to be working, you can always choose again. I realize when you see differently, things will be different and when you can be different (and you can), you will see differently. This changes your experience of life, which impacts how you treat people and how they treat you. If you want things different, be different, the choice is always yours. See life that way, be that way, and your answers will find you. With this way of thinking, I was able to move from having a positive attitude to living a powerful life. My life would evolve using the authority of choice and possibility.

I had made progress in my professional life, but in my personal life I was still holding on to less than loving feelings toward people I love and my closest family members. Although this unforgiving nature had allowed me to live a somewhat fulfilled professional life, my life as a whole was still lacking.

There were still less than loving feelings from my childhood that I was holding on to which represented *the Rest of Me* and did not allow *the Best of Me* to shine through. The young fellow from the projects felt good about the progress he had made, but still sometimes focused not on the progress, but how far he still had to go.

Although the quality of life I was experiencing had improved tremendously, there was still work to do, so my search for hidden treasures continued.

I had gotten caught up in how wonderful the new path was, changing me so much so that I was simply marveling in the occurrences. They were coming at such a pace that I lost sight of things that may have been going on that were not representative of my *Best Self* when it came to my personal life.

I was still holding my twin brother responsible for our falling out in the late 70's or early 80's; some 20 or so years before. I had not let go of the headaches from the past. I did not realize this but seemed to be stuck.

It's fascinating to see how I had applied the living principles to one area of my life and not to all. I was practicing the principles but not across the board.

As I stated previously, as an adult I have always considered myself a lifelong learner. In 1998 or 1999 my twin brother, Marvin, tried to introduce me to Landmark Education, an educational corporation which offered courses that were known to make life changing differences in people's lives around the world. He had been introduced to Landmark and felt the experience had brought quality to his life. My initial attitude was my life is fine. His life might have been broken; however, I was not interested in what he was saying or claimed about his educational experience. I was still holding on to some residue from the fallout we had some 20 years prior!! When it came to him, it seemed easier for me to express myself from the realm of my lower self, *the Rest of Me*, than from my higher *Self*, which matters most or *the Best of Me*.

It was definitely the most difficult relationship for me to practice living the principles aligned with *the Best of Me*, which had surely transformed my life.

It wasn't until a year later, while I was involved in a different educational course that Vikki, a classmate and I were talking about our personal and professional goals. She mentioned Landmark Education as a worthwhile program. Coming from her it sounded more like advice from someone I respected, someone who was supportive. Whereas, when my brother shared, my attitude was more like "I don't need anything positive happening in my life coming from him; especially since he wasn't sharing anything positive when we were having our differences of opinion and falling out some 20 years before."

Oh, how I had held onto the "I was right and you were wrong" mindset, a sign of living from *the Rest of Me* and not from *the Best of Me* for sure.

However, because it was my classmate's suggestion I did seek out and ultimately enrolled in a class through Landmark Education. I stayed involved and took other courses over the span of a couple of years. Through my involvement with Landmark and the living principles that I was already practicing, I experienced more life changing and transforming moments. I definitely had a much needed breakthrough in communication with my wife, another important person in my life. You see we were married five years earlier, and although it had been a happy, wonderful, and peaceful life together; it was not without some challenges or obstacles.

It had become apparent that we got along as husband and wife, however, communication between us could use some work. On Fridays I would drop her off and pick her up from work to spend scheduled time together either to have dinner or take in a movie. However, not much conversation seemed to take place during this time.

After a while, in my head I simply blamed my wife for our lack of communication, an indication of me living from *the Rest of Me* and not *the Best of Me*. I was more into blaming her instead of claiming full responsibility in resolving the matter. (Lost)

Although I was living and reaping the benefits of living a life I loved, doing what I truly loved to do professionally, I was guilty of holding on to a common way of thinking, living and being. I was living in the realm of right and wrong, needing to be correct about her being wrong, and the reason for our lack of communication.

This way of living took me back some 15 years before my first conscious awareness of the transformation that took place in my life. The lack of communication wasn't causing any real problem in the marriage, but I had developed an overtone of "Something's missing and it's just the way it is." I was convinced that the absence of communication between us had everything to do with her and nothing to do with me. In my mind, I had tried to communicate much too often, but to no avail. On top of that, men had been stereotyped as not being good at or much interested in expressing themselves in relationships, and I knew in my mind I was quite the opposite. I was willing to share my thoughts and feelings most of the time. I had come to the conclusion, she was the problem and that was just the way it was, and no need to press the issue.

I had my job doing what I loved to do, so I wasn't going to turn our absence of communication into some large size blow up. If she didn't know how or want to communicate, we could still love each other in other ways, maybe one day she would come around was my thinking; "just one day maybe." *(Lost and Seeking)*

We didn't argue and fight, like you might hear about couples doing; so the lack of communication was okay with me. Considering the freedom and joy of living in a space of happy and strong, day in and day out professionally, somehow I didn't mind living in the realm of right and wrong in my personal relationship.

A typical Friday evening family night for the two of us would consist of me picking her up from work, on our way to a customary Friday night movie. I'm out in front of her job waiting for no more than a couple of minutes. She opens the car door; and as she gets in the car. "Hey, how was your day?" "Okay" was her typical response. Silence as we drove off heading to the movies. No talking for the next 15 or 20 minutes while on our way. I just drove and wondered to myself what's going on with her; it's the same old same old silent treatment. How is it, that someone could pretty much not see you all week, and not have anything to say when you did come together? Our sleep schedules were different and because of it we would by-pass one another during the work week and basically see each other on the weekend. Friday after she got off work would generally be the first time really being together. I thought we should have a lot to talk about when I picked her up on the way to the movies. But that was not the case. On a few occasions after asking "how was your day?" and her standard response of "okay;" I would ask; "what do you mean okay?" At first, to my surprise I would get the same response, but unfortunately, after a while I just accepted her same old answer. Mentally, I would just shake my head in disbelief, but ultimately accepted the fact that she just didn't want to talk with me. I didn't know what was wrong, why she didn't have anything or much to say. I decided "it's just the way it is."

After completing my first course in Landmark I achieved the much needed breakthrough about truly understanding communication. I saw it differently; begun approaching it in another way; and conversely experienced talking with my wife like we had not done in the previous five years of our marriage. *(Acceptance)*

My definition of communication had been I talk, you talk, I talk, you talk, a back and forth type of thing. Listening as a part of communication was not at the forefront of my definition. Through an experience in the Landmark course, I uncovered listening as a form of communication, when prior to that I always thought talking was how you communicated. I didn't realize the importance of listening and how listening was a key ingredient in successful communication.

As a result, I was able to stop speaking and began listening to what my wife had to say. From this I was able to get more information from her, a greater understanding of her, and where she was in her thinking. This happened because I stop talking and allowed her to talk. It was a fascinating experience and another breakthrough for me in my life. An upgraded form of communication, oh what a relief it was! It really made a difference. *(Change and Attainment)*

Remember now; this was the education that my brother had tried to introduce me to at least a year and a half prior to me going. I wasn't able to see the blessing he saw and wanted for me. My definition of who he was, and who I was, prevented me from accepting his advice. I was stubbornly still stuck in the past, stuck in the pain, stuck in the realm of right and wrong; a description of *the Rest of Me*.

Three years later I was ranting and raving to friends, family and anyone else who would listen about how wonderful the experience and Landmark Education was. I enthusiastically shared how it had brought communication to my marriage, something which had been missing for so long. It brought a new awareness about choice, the power of choice, and how we treat that power affects our lives. I almost missed it, by living my less than *Best* kind of thoughts and feelings toward my twin brother.

I'm grateful for *the Best of Me* journey and path I was on, practicing and traveling through life. So many other wonderful things had come to me over the years that supported me in sharing and supporting love, doing what I truly loved to do. Was this another one of those experiences of support the *Universe* provides when you're living in accordance with *Universal Principles* and natural laws or living *the Best of You*? I believe so.

In hind sight, I realized I had been holding on to some anger and upset in the back of my mind toward my brother, and I lived stuck in the realm of right and wrong as it related to communication with my wife. All the while I was making a conscious effort to keep *the Best of Me* at the forefront of my thinking when it came to my work, career and life in general.

I came to understand that the tug of war between *the Best of Me* and *the Rest of Me* is an ongoing, day in and day out occurrence. In order to experience *the Best of Life*, it is so important to make the conscious choice to live *the Best of You*.

After riding the wave of my Landmark Education experience, the new found awareness of communication and choice in my life, an unexpected idea and concept of *"WhoyouBeing?"* came to me.

What did it mean? What was it for? How could or would I use it? In the upcoming chapter I will explain more and share how it led to the development of *Best Self Living*, the program and the inspiration for this book.

CHAPTER 7

WHOYOUBEING?

As I mentioned earlier, my life experience had definitely taken a turn for the better, and that better became an ongoing occurrence. What happened one morning in the summer of 2010 was an introduction to another insightful way of living. Another addition to the gifts I had received on the Path arrived. After 25 years of teaching, this new addition changed the way I taught, thought and ultimately lived. It grew to be a far greater influence in my life than I could have ever imagined.

On this particular day, while taking a shower, the question *"WhoyouBeing?"* came to me. What did it mean? What was it for? How could or would I use it?

For a few days I didn't have a clue, then one day during a tennis lesson I used the question to get a tennis student to stay focused on a particular skill, goal and way of handling it. I recognized how effective it was and what evolved from that, transformed my teaching and my life.

I was always looking to improve as a teaching professional or coach. With the introduction of the question *"WhoyouBeing?"* my teaching experience became less stressful. My teaching experience had not been very stressful in the first place, however, whatever amount of stress I was experiencing prior to *"WhoyouBeing?"* decreased substantially. I realized how much I had been taking credit and responsibility for the rapid progress of my students or the slow or lack of progress my students had made over the years.

I learned my teaching had been more about me and control, than educating my students. I became aware of how attached I had been to how I was perceived as a teaching pro in the tennis community. When students of mine learned quickly and did well, I looked good as a teaching pro. If they took too long to learn, in my mind, they diminished my credibility as a professional.

I ultimately realized that prior to including *"WhoyouBeing?"* in my teaching, that on some occasions if my students and I had already gone over corrections or adjustments that needed to be made, and for some reason or another they did not maintain focus and execution of what had been shared, after a while I would become somewhat annoyed.

I had defined myself as a *Kingdom Kid*; here to share and support love. This allowed me to maintain my composure and resist outward expression of my temporary less than loving feelings.

However, I recall feeling and sometimes communicating that I was the teaching pro with so many years of experience, and if you came to me as a student, it was your duty and responsibility to listen and do as I asked you to do.

I felt if you did not listen to what I had ask you to do, to a certain extent you were ignoring me, my experience and my ability to teach and this was not acceptable. You would either receive a tongue lashing for not listening, wasting yours and my time, or I would send you off to work on a particular skill on your own as some form of punishment. This would be done with the deepest intent to share and support love with you at the same time.

As a result of the *"WhoyouBeing?"* question and catchphrase, I was able to witness my students achieve better results at a higher rate, and came to realize how much more freeing and enjoyable it was to teach. So "how is this?" you might ask. Through the process I learned more about the deficiency in my previous ways of teaching. I recognized how control of others had been a common practice and this represented awareness of a better way. I came to understand what made it better, and was able to eliminate the unnecessary, contradictory verbiage I had been using over the years.

After a typical summer evening of my weekly Wednesday class, I was having a private lesson with a student named Sonya. "Okay Sonya, get your toss up higher" I suggested. "When you get your toss up higher your serve goes in, and when you let your toss get low you're serving into the net." As I walked to the other side of the court to pick up some balls I looked back and there she was again, with a low toss on her serve, and with the ball going into the net rather than over the net into the service box. "Sonya" I repeated "get your toss up higher." Then it hit me try *"WhoyouBeing?"* so I did.

I called her over, we gathered up balls that had been scattered around the court and then we began. "So this is what I want you to do, toss the ball up, a little higher okay?" She did. "Okay right there, that's good, that's a three foot toss. "Where you were tossing the ball before is too low, that's like a one foot toss." "When you make a three foot toss, you get your serve in; when you make a one foot toss, you hit it into the net." "So, who I want you to be for the next five minutes is a three foot toss." "Can you do that?" she replied, "yes." "So, for the next five minutes you will be a three foot toss?" "What does that mean?" I asked and suggested "It means you will toss your ball up three feet on your serve to hit it in the service box." "So can I count on you for that?" She replied "yes." She tossed her ball up three feet and hit her serve into the service box. I smiled at her, I smiled to myself, it was an "aha" moment for me.

I walked to the other side of the court, looked back and observed a couple times that she didn't toss her ball as high and instead of responding like I had responded for so many years with "get your ball up higher" I simply said *WhoyouBeing?*" she replied "a three foot toss," I smiled and said "okay."

As I walked and picked up balls, oh what a relief it was, I had stumbled upon a way to support my students and their tennis advancement without taking responsibility and credit for their choices.

Using *WhoyouBeing?*" allowed me to see if she would choose a three foot toss or not, not whether or not she was listening to me. She would have success if she chose the three foot toss instead of the lower one foot toss. The choice was up to her and I was there to remind her of the choice she had made by simply asking *WhoyouBeing?*" Once identified the desired result or goal, the desired way to accomplish it, she made the declaration or commitment to be that, and I was there to be supportive not responsible.

Once she declared her effort, when she didn't affirm it, I was able to remind her simply by asking her a question, instead of repeatedly telling her what to do.

This technique truly provided me with the awareness of how much we can take responsibility and credit for other people's actions and in doing so wear ourselves down. However, when we give others the credit and responsibility for what's truly theirs, we lift the weight off of our shoulders and allow ourselves to be free, while supporting others in being responsible for what's rightfully theirs, be it success or failure in whatever they pursue.

After my experience with Sonya and a three foot toss, I used the *"WhoyouBeing?"* technique in my classes and was amazed at the results. Weight had been lifted from me, and the freedom to enjoy the experience of teaching at a level I had not done before began. When using *"WhoyouBeing?"* I gave the responsibility of choice to my student and was able to play the role of support and instructor, who I intended to be all along.

Not too long after that, I imagined if *"WhoyouBeing?"* worked for my tennis, could it work off the court in my life as well. If playing tennis is a skill and living life is a skill, I thought to myself, why not? I started looking at all the ways it made a difference in my teaching, the ingredients involved and how far reaching the question could be used. How much ground could be covered using this simple yet powerful and profound question? So I started practicing on myself with it. The *"WhoyouBeing?"* question and catchphrase was a way to encourage me to remember, and in doing so became a tool I used to keep myself on task, target and on time. I got really excited.

I started using *"WhoyouBeing?"* as a declaration, written or spoken to represent how I would be or behave throughout my day. A typical *"WhoyouBeing?"* declaration might be "I'm being peaceful, pleasant, and productive", followed by *"WhoyouBeing?"*

I wanted to stay focused on how I would show up on the planet each day, and the state of mind I'd maintain when I encountered people, situations or circumstances, whether they were desirable or undesirable. Otherwise, without being mindful or prepared, I could in some way or another handle my life experiences carelessly which could lead to objectionable behavior or results. I wanted to be proactive when it came to dealing with life situations, instead of being reactive to the issues and problems of the world.

My initial idea about sharing my declarations with others was to get them to ask me who I'm being as often as they asked me how I was doing or feeling. I wanted to have a support team that would encourage me to remember who I am, and to show up on the planet accordingly. This simple question would bring my attention to, or back to, my goal or desired result, which at the highest level was to be my *Best of Self.* This was such an invaluable question and catchphrase.

The idea that I could use this question as a reminder in any area of my life, whether it was work, business or play intrigued me to no end.

I started with a few friends and family and then any and everybody in my contact list were receiving a *"WhoyouBeing?"* declaration from me at least two or three times a week. The response I got back encouraged me to continue sharing this.

Some examples of declarations I shared over the years with my associates, friends and family are:

a) "I'm being peaceful, pleasant and productive . . . *'WhoyouBeing?'*"

b) "I'm being *Love or Lesson*, here to count my blessings and not to be stressing about life . . . *'WhoyouBeing?'*"

c) "I'm being faith, strong, and worry free; a shoulder of support and a hug when in need . . . *'WhoyouBeing?'*"

In sending these *'WhoyouBeing?'* declarations out, and that's exactly what I did, (send them out). I did not explain why I was sending them or what I was trying to accomplish with them. I simply wrote them out in the form of a text on my phone and sent them to almost everyone in my contact list.

Now mind you many of the people in my contact list I had not seen or spoken to in quite some time but they would still receive these unexplained declarations from me in a text. Some would respond with a declaration of their own, others with some sort of "I'm with you" response. Occasionally, I would get a "Who is this?", while some did not respond at all.

This was time consuming, it would take about 2 hours or so of my time, on the days I would send them. However, it was also fascinating to be engaged in a new awareness that I wanted to get out and share with the world; my world at the time.

I remember one day a former tennis partner of mine responded, "I'm being me."

For the many times that followed, she would provide that same response, "I'm being me." I was interested in her sharing some powerful descriptive way of being she would aspire to be that day, however "I'm being me" is what I got. I pondered her repeated response. I realized the question *"WhoyouBeing?"* spoke to many things and addressed various areas of one's life, but "I'm being me" did not speak to or focus on the growth or development I wanted to address by asking the question. I came to realize that there are so many quality aspects of us, some that support love and our greater good, and others that do not. My attempt was to identify those that do, and declare, focus and fuel them, while not giving energy to those that distract or destroy the love.

I gathered that space, place and time were aspects of who we are being, and one day I would speak to that. I would help clarify how we could use the question *"WhoyouBeing?"* to our overwhelming benefit.

When my life was transformed some 25 years earlier, I was being a *Kingdom Kid* (Child of God), here to share and support love, however the *"WhoyouBeing?"* question, and catchphrase which could be used to help transform lives was not a part of my vocabulary or living practice at the time. I was however, applying the same principle.

On Wednesday evenings at five o'clock I would teach Pee Wee tennis to a class of rambunctious four to six year-olds. I recalled how working with them on Wednesday evenings was different than teaching the adults, seniors or the teenagers I had in my tennis programs. Wednesday mornings, I would remind myself that "today is the day to carry my patience with me; I will need it dealing with the pee wees." So every Wednesday evening I would go to class prepared to be patient.

I was already being a *Kingdom Kid*; sharing and supporting love; however on Wednesdays, it required a little extra patience. So I would include patience as part of my way of being that evening.

Often, over the years I would run into parents of former pee wee students and they would say something to the effect of, "Coach Foreman I don't know how you did it; dealing with those kids and their energy." "You really did a great job and were so patient with them."

There was that word patience, that little something extra I would tell myself I needed on those Wednesday evenings. It sure came in handy. I guess after a while I believed I could be patient, and in believing I could, along with saying I would, assisted me in displaying the behavior of a patient person much like when I believed I was a shy teenager. Saying so definitely supported me in behaving that way.

The cycle or circle of patience continued.

If that was the case then why would it be any different now declaring qualities I would carry through the day affirming and reaffirming?

In 2010, I was invited to fill in as coach for the girl's tennis team at Renaissance; a local high school where a tennis colleague of mine was coaching. He was scheduled to take off a couple of weeks that particular season to have some minor surgery done. The two weeks off turned into the entire season, so for that tennis season I was able to introduce the girls on the team to this *"WhoyouBeing?"* concept I had used with my students in my tennis classes. However, this time I was not only able to use it as a way to develop strokes but to establish and support the development of a mindset that I felt would provide the greatest opportunity for the girls on the team to excel on and off the court.

The following year my colleague offered me the opportunity to replace him as head coach permanently. I said yes and continued to share the *"WhoyouBeing?"* philosophy and used the team as a way to test and practice the concept.

I was informed by Mrs. Thomas, a parent who had been and still remained heavily involved with the tennis team, that the use and practice of *"WhoyouBeing?"* was having a positive impact with the girls on the team. She informed me that it was so much so that they were using it with each other outside of tennis, during school throughout the day.

Mrs. Thomas was also the President of the Parent Group at the school, and she enjoyed what was happening with the girls so much so that she asked if I would come and share my *"WhoyouBeing?"* concept at one of the Parent Group meetings.

After a few invites and some hesitation, a few months later I accepted and gave my first presentation on the *"WhoyouBeing?"* concept I had been sharing with the tennis team.

Although the presentation went pretty well, there was a part of me that felt something was missing and I had not yet figured out what it was.

I continued to work with the tennis team daily as well as text *"WhoyouBeing?"* declarations to the 300+ contacts in my cell phone.

The question *"WhoyouBeing?"* came to me, and I introduced it as a skill in tennis. However, the greatest gift the question provides is how it can be used to remind you to remember who you are at the highest level of your being. This is vital to you living *the Best of Life*. *"WhoyouBeing?"* can be applied for us at work, business or play. It reminds us mentally, emotionally, spiritually, socially, physically or financially to see and be our *Best of Everything*. Its use is unlimited and valuable in all aspects of life. Look at how valuable the awareness of your present state of mind or the focus of your attention can be in a moment's notice when asked *"WhoyouBeing?"* It could be the question to bring focus back to a strong and responsible place of good judgement. It is definitely valuable when prior to the question one is operating from a less than appropriate feeling or emotion, heading down a path of later regret. It's what I had gone without when it came to my brother for 20 years, and what a shame.

A present state of mindful thinking is great for reinforcing *the Best of intention*, effort and practice regarding a job, goal, activity, project, relationship, life and living in general. *"WhoyouBeing?"* existence is based on supporting such a thing.

Given that awareness, how would I deal with one of the most devastating losses in our family? Nothing but God is the answer.

How do I apply the same principle or belief when in 2009, I lost my cousin Doug, a wonderful father, son and family member to a violent act of murder by someone who bore his child and was believed to love him? It was a bitter, bitter pill to swallow. Outside of the lost and all the pain our family had experienced or endured, I was led back to the same living Principle I had been practicing and accepting as my truth for so many years. If life is *Love or Lesson*, what could I learn from this because an expression of love was nowhere near in any shape, form or fashion?

It was some five years later before this case went to trial. The experience had the same feel and sense of tragic loss we see, hear or read about too often in this country on a day to day basis.

I prayed and asked over and over "what can I learn from this;" because no matter what we as a family felt about her, it would not bring Doug back. Even after she was found guilty and sentenced to life in prison, it didn't take away the fact that he was gone; had left here in such a tragic way and wasn't coming back. The pain of that reality remains. *(Lost and seeking)*

After the sentencing, something came to me that I had not noticed before. I realized that I had been asking people who they were being, in an attempt to encourage people to be positive instead of negative with their attitudes. I had been asking people who they were being, hoping to get them to take responsibility for the things they were responsible for, and to stop trying to control or take credit for that which they were not. The same thing I had done for so long teaching tennis, until the idea of *"WhoyouBeing?"* surfaced.

The response I got with this approach with my students was great but with others in general was minimal at most. Even though I knew it was a valuable way to enhance one's experience of life.

What came in a very big way was, the young lady, who took my cousin's Doug life, actually went to a friend of hers house, a short while later, to talk and discuss what happened, and so on. I realized that maybe just maybe, if she had been exposed to the *"WhoyouBeing?"* practice she could have been in communication with her friend before she decided to do what she did to Doug. In doing so, she could have been reminded of who she was at the highest level and how she was showing up at the time. With a shift in mind, the situation could have been handled totally different, in a more rational, civilized and loving way. My thinking was "If only it was already part of her way of being, what a difference it could have made that day."

Through a simple supportive question, you can be reminded of who you are, the power you have to choose, be, live and express as your true and highest *Self.* You can live at a level higher than your feelings. You can begin to develop the habit of asking yourself "what can I learn from this, so I can return from this to love," when your feelings are in a less than loving place.

I'm not suggesting that this is the easiest thing to do; especially when you don't have experience doing it. However, I am implying that it is definitely an alternative to accepting your less than loving feelings as who you are, and acting out accordingly.

We as a culture have done too many senseless things when we act out of our less than loving feelings. This is not who we are. We are more than our up and down feelings and emotions.

I've continued sharing the *"WhoyouBeing?"* practice however; instead of focusing on how wonderful life could be using the *"WhoyouBeing?"* question; I've now included how awful and terrible life is when we don't ask the question or practice being our *Best of Self.*

There's who you are, how you are, and who you choose to be. Your presence and experience in life depends upon your choice.
This has influenced the new chapter in my life; the basis for this book and the next chapter on *Best Self Living.* In it I will share how *"WhoyouBeing?"* the question, catchphrase and declaration evolved into the daily practice of *Best Self Living.*

"The mind is owned by the self and can make a hell of heaven or a heaven of hell." — *John Milton*

CHAPTER 8

BEST SELF LIVING

After a few years of using and sharing *"WhoyouBeing?"* as a workable idea and practice; in 2012, my contract of 20+ years with the city of Detroit ended. I decided to take the successful living philosophy I had used over the years in my professional and private life and create a program out of it. A program I could share with the rest of the world, which would allow me to continue doing what I love to do and provide a platform for the next professional chapter in my life.

Sharing and expanding the *"WhoyouBeing?"* idea into a program was my initial intent, but a critical part was missing.

Best Self Living emerged as the missing piece. The experience was another example of the growth and success I experienced by believing and living the principles I accepted for myself and life in my twenties, and continued with over the years.

When my contract with the city of Detroit was terminated, I went through a grieving period and could not believe how such a thing could happen to me. After all I had done for tennis in the city over the years to be laid off did not seem fair.

Once I accepted the fact that the city was no longer contracting my services, an alternative working opportunity appeared and I continued to provide tennis for the residents of Detroit. It was under a different umbrella but still in conjunction with the Recreation Department.

It took me a while but I came to realize that if I truly wanted to reach more people and share the living philosophy which had served me so well over the years, I could not continue to coach and teach tennis the same amount of hours I had. My time needed to be cut so I could give more time to my newest project.

For the previous 20+ years I had identified teaching tennis as the thing that I loved to do, and used it as a vehicle to share my living philosophy sporadically.

In 2014, after two additional years of contracting tennis with the city of Detroit Recreation Department through an outside organization, tennis ended again. I came to a space of acceptance and began to transfer my time and energy from the sport of tennis into my *"WhoyouBeing?"* program idea.

As I look back, I realize, if my contracts with the city had not been terminated, I most likely would still be teaching tennis and sharing my philosophy with the limited amount of people who played tennis in my classes and programs. Now instead, I get to share this wonderful way of being which has transformed my life with so many more.

I'm so glad I continued to align myself with the living Principle of doing what I truly loved to do; and accepted the *Universe* would support me and handle the details of how to make it happen.

After continuously introducing and sharing the idea of *"WhoyouBeing?"* I was asked to share it publicly with groups of people, and subsequently I did. I was excited to share but knew within me some key ingredient was not there yet. One day I was watching 60 minutes or a Dateline television episode about some form of violence going on across America, and in doing so *Best Self Living* presented itself. I blended it with *"WhoyouBeing?"* and the missing piece for sharing my recipe for happiness was formed.

It appeared to me that sharing the new possibility of living *the Best of You* without sharing the same old probability of living less than best or *the Rest of You* was not getting people's attention. I needed to share the agony of defeat, living from your Average and Worst Self, before the thrill of victory, living from your *Best Self*.

From this awareness a structured view of *Best Self Living* emerged, which helped paint a distinct picture of the different *Levels of Self*, while *"WhoyouBeing?"* provided the push, pull and presence to hold it all together.

I finally felt I had my recipe and response to the age old question I set out to get answered at the young age of 11, "what would it take for you to be happy in life?"

I was still involved in tennis and used my career as a vehicle to share my new found happiness recipe. I began to spend a significant amount of time developing it, because I was definitely excited, and wanted to share my insight with the rest of the world.

For teaching purposes I created three *Levels of Self*, each representing their own distinct characteristics and attributes, your *Best*, Average, and Worst *Self*. For the sake of this book *the Best of You* reflects your *Best Self*, and *the Rest of You* is a combination of your *Average* and *Worst Self*.

LEVELS OF SELF

BEST SELF:	AVERAGE SELF:	WORST SELF:
Purpose, Power, Peace and Passion	*Feelings, Emotions Likes & Dislikes*	*Hate, Anger & Fear*
Happy/Strong	**Right & Wrong**	**Don't Belong**
What Matters Most	**What Matters Least**	**What matters not**
Roles, Goals & Limitless Potential	*Problems, Faults & Present Capacity*	*Mindless, Senseless Acts*
INNER DRIVEN	**OUTER DRIVEN**	**POORLY DRIVEN**
Self Control Claim Responsibility	*Seeks to Control Blame Responsibility*	*Out of Control Lacks Responsibility*

The term *the Best of You* refers to you living the love, the *Christ*, the highest qualities of being. The term *the Rest of You*, refers to you living the less than loving, up and down feelings and emotions, led by symptoms of fear such as hate, anger, envy, jealousy and guilt. *The Best of You* is a living practice that moves you towards your finest or highest potential, while *the Rest of You* moves you away from it.

There are a wide range of characteristics and attributes that reside inside each and every one of us. We live our lives from the worst to the best of these characteristics and attributes.

A) There is a direct correlation between the characteristics, attributes and the *Level of Self* you live from and the experience of life you have.

B) If you want to experience *the Best of Life*, live from *the Best of You*.

C) If you want to see obstacles, setbacks and challenges as mere fuel to thrust you toward a life you want, a life you love, your greatness; then live from *the Best of You*.

When you're being your *Best Self* you're putting yourself in position to be *the Best of You* in every aspect of your life. However, without mindfully being your *Best of Self*, you can be the best businessman and a terrible husband or father. Without it, you can be the best mother, wife or daughter and a terrible employee, manager or employer. Be *the Best of You* and you will be your *Best* of whatever role, title or position you hold. In being so, your quality of life will be lifted.

For 20 years I was in and out with my brother, blocking money, riches, financial freedom from my life. "How was that?" you might say. Well, I came to realize later, what I didn't realize then, and that was, I saw myself as a good guy, and wanted to be seen as a good guy. At the same time, I was highly upset and angry with family but didn't want to be seen as a bad guy. I said I wanted to make lots of money, but lots of money seemed to elude me. Now mind you, some 15 or so years earlier, when I accepted the *Universal Principle* of doing what you truly love to do, and the *Universe* will support you in it, I also accepted another *principle* that states abundance is the natural state of the *Universe*, and if you are not experiencing abundance in your life it is because you are blocking it either consciously or subconsciously.

I had been so caught up being right about family being wrong and stuck in anger and judgmental feelings; I didn't realize how my way of being or level of thinking was blocking my financial wealth.

I was so committed to being a good guy, and remaining upset with my family at the same time. There was no way I was going to share my financial wealth with them when I got it. However, if I had it and didn't share it, there was no way in my mind I could be a good guy. So, standing strong in both of those convictions the only way I could still be a good guy was to not have a lot of money. That way I wouldn't have to share it. How limiting my thinking was, and we can be when we refuse to live from our *Best Self or Level of Best*. What nonsense, but it was the truth about me at the time.

It was more important for me to be right about him being wrong, than to see him and myself, whole and complete just the way we were, simply caught up in living from a lower *Level of Self*. Remember, you are not your behavior; your behavior is a mere reflection of the *Level of Self* you are accustomed to, and are living from at that time.

It took a while but, I did come to realize, that both my brother and I at the highest level are individualized expressions of *Love and Greatness*, here to share and support love doing what we truly love to do, while lovingly serving the greater good. I had been living lost, without sight, seeking to be found and regain some vision of the truth, my *Best of Self*.

Best Self is a skill, and practice makes . . . . better. Recognizing the various qualities and characteristics at each level, practicing the qualities of *Best*, and eliminating *the Rest*, can change your view and experience of life. It can raise your level of living, save lives, and help transform humanity. *(Awareness and Acceptance)*

Many if not most of us have grown up in a culture that lives in the realm of Right and Wrong, not Happy Strong. A cultural mindset led by what matters least over what matters most, blaming and shaming instead of framing and claiming responsibility. A society spent living in a realm supporting and reinforcing living from your lower *Level of Self.*

If you are ever going to live the happy, joyous, fulfilling life you were meant to live, seek education in the area of *Self.*

I was able to get mine through self-help, personal power, enrichment education, and Spiritual influence. We need to seek learning outside the traditional cultural education we've received over the years. Traditional education has not been set up or arranged to support us personally in living our highest good or well-being, individually nor collectively.

If our culture doesn't teach or speak *Best Self* language, we have to learn it on our own. Living without it can destroy us mentally, emotionally, spiritually, socially, professionally, physically and financially.

Best Self Living and *Level of Self* education's goal is to provide some understanding and peace that otherwise you would not have. With peace you are able to maintain what you have or accomplished. Without peace, you can lose everything in an instant.

Level of Self education helps assist you with looking at human behavior with compassion and understanding, a key ingredient in redeveloping a life of love. The greater your understanding of *Self*, the higher the *level of Self* you can live from. The *Levels of Self* chart provides some differences in how we show up. It helps to create a picture of what's possible. It provides a model for desirable and undesirable behavioral practice. It helps you to both ask and answer the question, "which experience of *Self* and life do I want?" Review a few stories on my journey and the results I got when living from my higher *Level of Self*. Observe how you might be living both *the Best* and *the Rest of You*.

If you could create the ideal world, what would it look like? What qualities would the people in your ideal world display? How about the ideal person, friend, mother, father, sister, brother, daughter, son, mate, neighbor, boss, employee, student, teacher, and so on?

Learn and practice being the qualities you want to see in your ideal world, the people you spend time or come in contact with. If you want to be happy, then be the qualities of happy now. If you want violence in the world to end, then be the qualities of peace. Be the qualities you want to see. How do you do that? By practicing those qualities as you navigate through your daily activities and encounters.

"WhoyouBeing?" declarations serve as an everyday way to build the skill and habit of being your *Best*, while serving the Greater Good. In living the ideal day, we get focused and start *Best Self Living* first thing in the morning. The daily practice involves waking up, to re-establish a meaningful purpose for your day and life. How so?

You wake up, pray, before you start your day, declare *"WhoyouBeing"*, and then be on your merry way. You want to re-establish who you are and why you're here, how you will show up, each and every day, all day. If you can develop this habit (and you can), so can everyone else including your family, friends and love ones.

To accomplish this individually and collectively we can literally change the wave of violence, abuse, and dysfunction in our society to a mainstay of purposeful, passionate, peaceful, powerful living of love and greatness. This is the true expression of who we are. You were created with the potential to express as your Best. However, unfortunately up until now many of us have forgotten who we really are. This forgetfulness has created a gap between our capacity and our potential to love. The experience of life we are having everyday supports us in closing that gap. How we respond to everything we encounter gives us an indicator to what *Level of Self* and capacity to love we are living from at that time.

It took me a while to get to *Best Self Living*. It was only by a strong desire, commitment to grow, finding an approach that worked and continual research and experience. Once the *Best Self Living*, *"WhoyouBeing?"* program came together, I began sharing and accepting speaking engagements and recognized I finally had my recipe and special sauce for being happy. Subsequently, I've been ready and willing to share it with any and everybody who is willing to listen.

MELVIN D. FOREMAN

Living *the Best of You* is living supported by the *Universe*; it's like swimming downstream with the current. Living *the Rest of You* is living supported by you and your effort without the support of the *Universe*; it's like swimming upstream against the current. This awareness helped me transition from thinking negatively to thinking positively, from positive thinking to powerful living.

The experience of *Best Self Living* is not one without opposition, competition or adversity. However with awareness and education, you recognize that opposition, competition, and adversity are actually meant to help you grow. When examined properly they help push you to get to, maintain and expand your *Level of Best*. They are intended to remind you to stay in constant contact with your *Source of Supply*, your highest *Level of Self*. They represent the test used to provide feedback to where you are mentally at any given moment. They are helpful feedback to alert you of your less than *Best* level of thinking.

In the next and final chapter I will remind you to remember who you are, who you're being, and to live your *Best* Now.

"The only person you are destined to become is the person you decide to be." — *Ralph Waldo Emerson*

CHAPTER 9

REMEMBER AND DON'T FORGET

We have grown up in a culture that focused so much on the mighty dollar, the pursuit of financial wealth and riches, that we as a people have been losing ourselves, family, friends, and loved ones in the midst. Violence, abuse and dysfunction, has run rampant in our society, communities, and families. We need to turn things around, or there will be nothing left worth spending our money on regardless of the amount we accumulated.

Living *the Best of You*, and not *the Rest of You*, is your basic life challenge. The goal or objective is for *the Best of You* to prevail.

My recipe for happiness stems from over 50 years of seeking, researching, learning and transformative experiences. The combination of education, lessons learned, personal transformation, the *Levels of Self*, and *"WhoyouBeing?"* grew into a daily practice of *Best Self Living*. *Best Self Living* helps you practice your *Best*, while *"WhoyouBeing?"* reminds you to remember you're *Best*. My hope is that you take and utilize what I've searched, researched and gathered, to assist you with your own transformative life. We have developed a cultural habit of creating assumptions and labels along with generalized conclusions about individuals and groups of people based on race, gender, citizenship or social status. We have prejudged one another based on less than loving feelings, expressions, or behavior, sourced by lack of awareness or misinformation about *Self*.

These cultural assumptions and generalizations not only fuel the existence of the unwanted, less than loving *Levels of Self*, but they also plant seeds and cultivates a belief system which perpetuates the demonstration and growth of a people totally different from who we really are.

This practice is based on made up stories, the lack of awareness and education of *Self*. This does not serve the greater good for all parties involved, which at the highest level of our being is intended. I'm suggesting we can put a stop to such habitual nonsense through awareness, acceptance and change, based on seeing and being different. If you're going to make up stories, make up stories that serve *the Best of Life* and the greater good, rather than *the Rest of Life* and the lesser evil.

THE WAY IT WAS

Although I grew up where and when I did, with the circumstances surrounding me as they were, I was still able to see and experience life differently.

At an early age I accepted "Seek and Ye shall find" as a truth I believed and would investigate.

I went from seeing the Worst in some to seeking the *Best* in all.

I FOUND A BETTER WAY

I changed my thinking and changed my way. I was brought to a new awareness, accepted it, and gave up complaining about what was lacking in my life, in exchange for being grateful for what I had.

NOTHING MORE POWERFUL THAN A MADE UP MIND

I made up my mind I would do my best to find a recipe for happiness, and I did. It was more important for me to find a better way than it was for me to accept what was considered the norm.

MY LIFE REDEFINED

We all have, at least a subconscious way of defining ourselves. A change in your personal definition will instantly change the talents you express, the behaviors you demonstrate, and the aspirations you pursue.

I realized I was a *Kingdom Kid*, child of God, here to share and support Love. Prior to that time, I was Melvin D. Foreman, a redhead African American twin from Detroit. Due to my new definition of *Self*, I looked at life differently as well as my role in it. The changed definition brought a different experience of life with it.

PRINCIPLE CENTERED LIFE OF LOVE

After redefining myself and my reason for being here, I allowed what I truly loved to do to lead me in my career choice. I am created from love, as love, here to share and support love in everything. Therefore, allowing the Principle of Love to decide my career choice made the utmost sense to me.

BIGGER THAN MY FEELINGS

I had made progress in my professional life, but in my personal life I was still holding on to less than loving feelings toward people I loved, and my closest family members.

My greatest awareness around feelings is, you may feel less than loving about someone or something however, feel what you feel but do not stop there; use those feeling and learn from them. Through insight gained from our feelings, we are able to learn more about how to expand our capacity to love, the real and truest reason we are here. "*Life is either Love or Lesson*, what can I learn from this so I can return from this to *Love*," is my ongoing prayer for growth. Allow this prayer to be answered and you are well on your way to growth and expansion beyond measure.

THE QUESTION, ANSWER AND KEY

"*WhoyouBeing?*" the signature question, answer and catchphrase used to promote, provoke and provide *the Best of You* at the most important time there is, the now moments of your life. You are a *Kingdom Kid*, a child of He who created the Heavens and the earth first; not male or female, black or white, your profession or possessions, position or social status. Too often we allow positions, titles and labels to separate or divide us, whereas, when we live who we really are, we use them to unite and provide for us.

LEVELS OF SELF

There are a wide range of characteristics and attributes that reside inside each and every one of us. We live our lives from the worst to the best of them. We're all capable of being our *Best*, *Average* or *Worst Self*, the difference is the level we choose. There is a direct correlation between the *Level of Self* you live from and the experience of life you have.

THROUGH IT ALL

I've come to use and see my daily personal and professional life as a learning institution for my experience of Best, and ongoing growth toward *Self Mastery*.

In Life:

1) Believe there's a better way.

2) Seek to find it.

3) Seek ye first the Kingdom.

In Love:

a) Don't blame or make them wrong

b) Use "look what I created" instead

c) Remember "I choose, I choose, I choose"

What I want to do with the book is to use it as a way to help eliminate the violence, abuse and dysfunction that has been taking place in the lives of so many people for so many years.

What I want the book to do for me is to give me access to the hearts and minds of a billion people, who will live their *Best of Self* and pass it on.

What I want you to do with the book is to read it, digest the information, apply it to your way of being, lifestyle, and lovingly pass it on.

What I want this effort to do for us all is, to give us a closer look and experience of *Self Mastery*, and a way for us to lovingly live our lives.

I hope I have shed some light on us as human beings both individually and collectively. A shift from the enormous amount of time spent focused on our outer self, to time used to explore and develop our inner *Self*.

I submit to you again, there is a direct correlation between the *Level of Self* you live from, and the experience of life you have.

My hope and want for us all, is to be our *Best Self*, have our *Best* days, live our *Best* life, master *Self*, and pass it on. If not you who, if not now when? May the rest of your life, be the best of your life.

If you want to live your *Best of Life*, live your *Best Now*. Thank You. *#WhoyouBeing?*

ABOUT THE AUTHOR

Melvin is a former tennis coordinator for the city of Detroit. He has spent 25 plus years working in Detroit as a teacher, coach, director, manager and tennis coordinator. He has worked with students from all walks of life, beginners to advance players, ranging in age from four to seventy four. He has trained at the world famous Nick Bollettieri Tennis Academy, worked for Arthur Ashe and has travelled the country honing his teaching skills. Melvin is a lifelong student of personal power, self-help and relationship work. He continues to search and research the works of many Spiritual and Personal growth thought leaders over the past century such as Dr. Wayne Dyer, Marianne Williamson, Deepak Chopra, Dale Carnegie, Stephen Covey, and Arnold Patent just to name a few. He also gives his work with Landmark Education much credit for the development of his living ideas, concepts and *Best Self Living* practice.

Melvin currently resides in Detroit with his lovely wife LaMonica and their amazing dog Koko. He is using his self-help, personal growth, empowerment project and business to partner with other businesses, organizations and institutions to one day create a cultural movement of *Best Self Living*. All of this stemmed from a lifelong dream of transitioning from living in a less than loving world of violence, abuse and dysfunction, to one day living in a joyful, rewarding, and powerful world of love. Melvin has a BA degree in Sociology, from Olivet College.

His education, research, experiences, lessons learned, his *Best Self Living* project and a strong desire to introduce himself and his work to those who were not familiar, led him to write this book.

For more information about Melvin and the fascinating work he's doing, you can email him at whoyoubeing@gmail.com, follow him on Facebook at facebook.com/whoyoubeing.wub, and Instagram or Twitter @whoyoubeing.

Made in the USA
Columbia, SC
01 October 2017